Energy Makeover®

A Conscious Way to Stay Young, Have Fun and Get More Done!

By

Betsy Muller

Energy Makeover® is a registered trademark of The Indigo Connection, LLC

Back cover photo by David Hebble

Book design and layout by Perseus Design

ISBN 978-1-935723-42-4

Printed in the United States of America

First Printing: 2011

Contents

To George, my loving husband and best friend.

Acknowledgements

I am blessed to have been nurtured, influenced, befriended and supported by many special people who have helped me to grow in consciousness.

I offer a special thank you to my parents, Clyde and Gail Bartter, who have always given me a safe and loving place to thrive. You have taught me to embrace the arts, be curious, love nature, read voraciously, be open to new ideas and to believe in the kindness of people from all over the planet. Mom's love for anemone flowers has inspired me to use these glorious blooms as the visual image for my book cover.

My children, Dan and Mandy, have taught me to take life balance and energy self-care very seriously. You showed me the value of an Energy Makeover® before it had a name. Thank you for warming my heart each time you ask for my coaching or advice.

I appreciate my sisters, Amy and Suzanne. We are lucky to live in the same town and it is comforting to know we are close and there for each other if help is ever needed.

I am grateful to my clients, too numerous to mention individually, for allowing me their sacred trust. Thank you for helping me become a more compassionate and humble healer. You are the reason Energy Makeover® exists.

To all of the friends, teachers and spiritual leaders I have met through the Association for Comprehensive Energy Psychology (ACEP): from the moment I met so many of you in Switzerland in 2001, I knew this was my home. A special thank you goes to the leaders who developed the certification program, whom I honor as mentors and friends: David Gruder; Dorothea Hover-Kramer; Larry Stoler; and Greg Nicosia. You gave me the ethical framework as well as the knowledge I needed to apply energy healing in my coaching practice. Gratitude to the generous board members and leaders in this field who have become my dear friends: Meryl Beck; Maria Becker; Melinda Connor, John Deipold; Donna Eden; David Feinstein; Tapas Flemming; John Freedom; Mandy Freger; Mary Hammond; Lynn Karjala; Jim Klopman; Tina Craig; Lori Leyden; Robin Masci; Phil Mollon; Midge Murphy; George Pratt; Carol Ann Rowland; Bob Schwarz; Mary Sise; Carole Stern; and Debby Vajda.

Thank you to Sherri Tenpenny, DO, and the staff of OsteoMed II for opening the door that allowed me to understand the role of energy in healing. Your friendship, kindness and all that I learned while working with you has been a blessing.

To Barbara Stone, for all that you have helped me understand about the human soul as my certification consultant and friend. Thank you for helping my light to shine even brighter.

Special thanks to Gary Craig, founder of Emotional Freedom Techniques. Your gift of EFT to humanity and sincere interest in helping others makes you my hero.

Thank you to my editor, Marcia Santore, for her professional assistance polishing and formatting my words.

To the generous volunteers who offered their time and sharp eyes for editing and feedback: Karen Brown, Nancy Coveleskie, Bert Fellows, Madeleine Holm, Pat Kugli, Beth Muellauer, Tracy Ols, Karen Poltrone and Jayne Sulser.

Appreciation goes to the expert coaches, authors, healers and leaders who have shown me how to build my professional image, platform, media presence, and business confidence in the spotlight:

Jane Ehrman, Mary Giuseffi, Steve Harrison, Diane Helbig, Les and Fran Hewitt, Ann McIndoo, Cheryl Richardson, Dawn Waldrop and Maryam Webster.

To the women of the Indigo Connection who have attended my meetings, events and retreats: thank you for your open minds, loving hearts and for supporting your sisters in personal development.

To my special girlfriends Rachel, Sue, Claire, Georgi, Cathy, Connie, Kim, Ann, Roseann, Dianna, Betsy (TOB) and Carmel, who have eagerly responded to dozens of invitations to *escape to magical places.*

To my husband, George, thank you for the unconditional love, friendship and joy you bring to my life. Your expertise as my "graphics guy" is priceless too. You and I have something magical.

Last but not least, I thank God, the source of the abundant energy available to heal and guide us all.

Introduction

"In every culture and in every medical tradition before ours,
healing was accomplished by moving energy."
Albert Szent-Gyorgyi, Nobel Laureate in Medicine

I distinctly remember a time when truth about my life purpose hit me right between the eyes—and it terrified me. I was in the middle of a guided imagery session in the office of my friend and colleague Janie Ehrman. I had drifted into a lovely relaxed state and felt myself fully connected to my wise inner advisor.

It was all going so well until Janie posed this question to my quieted mind, "Who are you?" she asked. Suddenly I heard a familiar voice reply, "I am a spiritual leader."

The instant my mind heard those words, I broke into a violent burst of tears. When Jane eventually inquired as to what was going on, my shaken voice replied, "I don't want to do that!" Unfortunately, I also knew deep inside that my wise inner advisor was telling the truth. I wasn't ready to accept that truth! I was unable to see the connection between the stressed out, unhappy woman who was sitting in the recliner that day and the leader I was destined to be. I thought, "Who would ever want to follow a stressed-out woman who was frantically struggling to get through each day with a fake smile on her face? How could a practical, rational, middle-aged woman with over 25 years of solid business management experience, an MBA and a chemistry degree start life over again as a spiritual leader? What kind of business was that?"

I realize today that my fears had to do with the word spiritual. I had somehow confused spiritual leadership with preaching and religion—things I never wanted or intended to do. What I had failed to recognize at that time was that SPIRIT IS ENERGY. When energy moves, spirit awakens! That was the kind of spiritual leader I was evolving to be through the Energy Makeover.

My energy began moving and my soul became activated emotionally and spiritually in 2001 when I first began practicing energy self-care techniques after attending a conference in Switzerland. There was an attractive glow to conscious living and it was a quality I wanted to nurture for myself and share with others.

I will admit that my Energy Makeover® transformation happened gradually back in 2001. I began studying Emotional Freedom Techniques (EFT), Touch for Health, Reiki, Neurolinquistic Programming (NLP) and a variety of other healing modalities on weekends. I also attended workshops and became an ordained non-denominational minister. Most of my early transformation involved working on me, examining how energy self-care created ease in my daily life. The more I used it, the easier everything became. Unfortunately, by the end of 2004, I had nearly stopped using the energy self-care techniques that I knew worked so well for me. I had let my job as general manager of a busy group medical practice and family demands steal my precious time and energy. My stressed body and fragile emotional state were screaming for a change.

I quit my job in early 2005, took a few months to reclaim clarity, and soon announced the creation of my new coaching practice. Through speaking and group seminars, I gained confidence as a healer and began attracting a combination of business and energy coaching clients. Eventually I became certified as an Energy Coach, EFT Practitioner and ACEP Energy Health Practitioner.

I intended to publish this book over five years ago, but kept putting it off because I was scared. The excuses I gave myself were endless. I rationalized my reluctance by telling myself that I was not yet experienced enough as an expert, healer, leader or coach to teach anyone what I knew to be true. Frankly, it came down to the fact that I was not ready to endure the criticism that I feared would come from sharing my truth in a way that defied the mainstream logic I had embraced for so many years.

Time, experience and what I know as the grace of God has changed me and allowed me to heal that fear and reluctance. Years of attending conferences, integrating new approaches and witnessing the healing transformation of my clients has been an empowering journey. This time of transformation in my own life has allowed me to see that life need not be such a struggle and that there are incredible opportunities for living in greater health, abundance and joy simply through the awareness and application of energy self-care. I am ready to humbly and honestly share what I know.

This book presents and builds upon approaches that have been carefully formulated and are in wide practice. I have not attempted to back the principles and methods I present with scientific support but want you to know that ample research on these techniques exists and has been accelerating in the past few years.* I have, in writing *Energy Makeover*, drawn primarily on my personal experimentation and my experiences working with hundreds of clients.

In the Appendix, I offer a listing of books and references to allow those who enjoy deeper study to explore the existing wealth of information available. This book reflects my belief that the most powerful examples of energy self-care come from your own personal experiences. You may enjoy reading, but the best part comes through feeling as you practice the concepts in *your* world.

I have been trained in science and have great respect for it, yet I also realize that science has a very hard time measuring subjective feelings and miracles. I often tell my clients and colleagues, "God doesn't like to be measured!" One of my most beloved teachers and cofounder of the Association of Comprehensive Energy Psychology, David Gruder, PhD, provided some important advice during my ACEP certification. He asked all of us to remain in a state of "enlightened stupidity." What he meant by this was that if you think you know it all, you will always be wrong. It is far better to be curious and open. While I don't like the idea of being stupid, I adore that enlightenment is the goal.

---

* Visit www.energypsych.org or www.eftuniverse.com and click on "research"

The day that I first uttered "spiritual leader" was a turning point that has taken me to where I am today and why I need to share what I know with you. You see, I have transformed my fear, healed my reluctance and realized that I am an eternal soul who mindfully chose this human life experience as a spiritual leader to make a difference. I have realized that leaders excel when they are creative, curious, open, balanced, enthusiastic, healthy, youthful and intuitive. I also recognize that using social media and modern technology, and having a polished, youthful image when working with the media are important tools that leaders must not fear and instead embrace with a positive attitude. Energy Makeover® addresses all of these things. Life in these times is complicated but also very exciting.

You may be attracted to this book because you are someone who is curious about living life to its fullest, just as I am. Like me, you might also worry that getting older and taking care of the commitments you've already made to others is keeping you from fully manifesting your mission. Your soul may be feeling trapped, blocked or restricted, too. It is my intention that this book will help you live with greater energy, purpose and ease. What I share with you will also help you appear younger than your years and add a kick to your step. The concepts in this book can help you to stay young, have fun and get more done—no matter how old you are or when you begin.

I don't claim to hold all of the answers for you, but through this book I will share a variety of discoveries that will allow you to experience your own unique Energy Makeover®. This makeover will activate the transformation of your physical experience, emotional health and a more powerful connection to everyone and everything. As this happens, your body may heal as you attract resources and find new opportunities for your talents. Spiritual leaders need not worry about leading alone. An army of enlightened leaders is emerging to protect and support one another as part of our mission. This book is my way of helping you navigate this exciting time with ease and in your own unique way. Our unique abilities and experiences give each of us a place in our Divine Creator's plan.

If you know of a curious seeker ready for a positive shift, please do your part by sharing this book with them as well. Please also share your stories of healing and empowerment with me. Know this is just the beginning of an amazing adventure we take together.

With love,
Betsy Muller
August 2011

Important Note: While the self-care practices that you will learn by reading Energy Makeover® have produced remarkable results for the author and her clients, readers are cautioned that these practices are considered to be in the experimental stage. Practitioners and the public must take complete responsibility for the use of the self-care practices outlined in this book. Betsy Muller is not a licensed health professional and offers Energy Makeover® as a certified personal coach, energy health practitioner and ordained minister. Please consult with a qualified health practitioner regarding your use of Energy Makeover® practices.

Chapter 1

Tuning In

"As you walk and eat and travel, be where you are.
Otherwise you will miss most of your life."
Buddha

What is Energy?

Energy is not something we're taught to understand very well in Western culture, yet it is something we experience every day of our lives. We can relate to terms like low energy, energy vampires and energy drain, yet somehow we're oblivious to what it takes to have optimal energy ourselves.

Energy is everywhere. Physics has demonstrated that energy cannot be created or destroyed. It simply transforms. Your body is energy. So is your food, water, the air you breathe and all the material things you want, have and love. Your thoughts and emotions are also energy. We live in a sea of energy, sending and receiving signals from every direction. Energy is not something to be feared or worried about. Rather it is something each of us can harness and use as a way to make life more pleasant.

Energy is what connects all living things. When we tap into energy as a way of being, we create unlimited opportunities for productivity, fun, spirituality, creation, better relationships and optimal health. If you are wondering if God is energy, my answer to that would be an enormous, unequivocal YES.

Some words for energy that you may have heard before include chi, prana, life force, spirit and ki. Think about how you already know and experience energy right now and don't limit yourself. You can start having a whole new awareness of everything as you take on an even greater understanding of energy.

Energy Moves and Flows

Energy is not only part of everything and everyone, it is moving and flowing. Just like a flowing stream or a gust of wind, energy is moving around you and inside of you all the time. When your internal energy flow is constricted, blocked or constrained from moving through your body, your health and organ systems may suffer. Ancient cultures have recognized the benefit of promoting the balance and flow of the body's energy through practices such as acupuncture, qi gong, yoga and tai chi for thousands of years. Energy that is freely moving and flowing is a natural, healthy and balanced state.

Your Unique Bandwidth

Everything is energy but you are unique, separate and you have your own energetic fingerprint. You have an energy field that surrounds you. You have a unique energetic signal that you send out into the world that you live in. Your unique energy is an invisible message that people feel and understand in some way when they are near you or when they speak to you over the phone. It's not just your voice or how you look. It is the essence of you, the frequencies you radiate and all that you are right now in this present moment.

Ever wonder why you gravitate toward certain people or are repulsed by others? That's bandwidth. Like attracts like. So even if you don't realize it, your thoughts, beliefs, experiences and energy field are attracting the life that you are living right now. Your frequency isn't stuck in one place but rather flows with your choices and experiences. The exciting thing about your energy is that it is dynamic— changing all the time. You have the power to change your thoughts, your frequency and also your ability to attract what you need, want and love.

Be aware of your energy with respect to that unique bandwidth concept. Bandwidth describes all that you are, all that you're attracting, all that is like you and all that you have the power to serve. Remember, you are unique. You carry a unique set of frequencies within your bandwidth of energy that serve to connect you with everything you encounter.

Your Energetic Senses

Think about your senses as one of the most amazing ways you already experience energy with your physical body. You are able to hear sounds, see colors, recognize patterns, feel soft breezes, taste wonderful foods and smell aromas. You may also find that you have heightened sensitivities in one or more of these senses. Pay attention to that because it can be a source of valuable guidance when used with intention.

I laugh when I remember one of my earliest energy awareness experiences back in 2001 when I attended my first energy psychology conference in Switzerland. At that point in time I was not an energy practitioner. I was oblivious to what my energy senses were telling me. I felt very inadequate walking into my first workshop with practitioners who seemed to be so far ahead of me in their ability to sense, intuit and be energetic healers.

As this workshop began, we were asked to make a big circle. The leader of the workshop, Meryl Beck, explained that she would create this invisible ball of energy between her two palms, and that in just a minute we were going to start passing this ball of energy across the circle to each other.

I remember sitting there thinking, "How am I going to fake this?" I really didn't understand energy at all at that time. I didn't think that I had any abilities with respect to sensing it, feeling it, receiving it or sending it. I sat there totally stressed out wondering if I could pull this off in this room full of experts. Soon the invisible energy ball started going around the room. As I watched, the others around the circle acted like they were getting it. They were sending and receiving. Everybody was laughing except me. I was sitting there dreading the moment I'd be selected to receive and getting more and more nervous with each passing moment.

Eventually the time came when I saw the woman across the circle lock her eyes on me. My gut churned as I realized that the energy was going to be heading my direction in any second. I braced myself and smiled tentatively. As the woman released that ball of energy in my direction, I instinctively brought my hands up in front of me to catch it.

What happened next took me completely by surprise. You see, I was hit by a ball of energy right in my heart as my hands went up. Oh my goodness, I felt it! It was as if the wind had been knocked out of me. It was an intense wave that vibrated through my whole body. Suddenly, I began sobbing in front of all these people I didn't know. I had not expected to feel anything, expected that I'd have to fake it, yet now found myself completely startled and overwhelmed with emotion.

As I sat there choking back the tears, Meryl looked at me with compassion. She was willing to give me a few seconds to get my act together. It seemed like eternity. Eventually she said, "Betsy, it's your turn. You have to send the energy now." I looked up and exclaimed through my tears, "I can't. I'm crying!" She shook her head and said, "Nope, you have to send it." It was then that a wave of new panic came over me again as I thought to myself, "How do I send energy?" I'd just received it but I had no idea how to send it. I'd only watched how all the other people had done it.

I picked up my palms as if I was holding an imaginary ball of energy, because that's what my little head was telling me I was holding. I looked across the room to the nicest, sweetest, kindest person I could find and lobbed that ball of energy in her direction. You know what? She caught it. And the minute she caught it, I could tell she felt it!

Experiencing the intensity of energy for the first time in my life, when I least expected it, was quite a thrill. By the end of that day, I had enjoyed my first experience with Emotional Freedom Techniques (EFT) and had witnessed Donna Eden's demonstration of several practices in Energy Medicine. By the end of that week, I had taken a spoon bending workshop and spent an entire day participating in a full-day seminar with Donna Eden and David Feinstein, PhD, that gave me an even deeper affection for Energy Medicine. I was convinced that these Energy Psychology practitioners were definitely onto something. I was especially impressed that they were such kind people willing to reach out to me as a beginner. Their absence of ego impressed me considerably and I knew I had found a new professional home where I could connect with them again, The Association for Comprehensive Energy Psychology (www.energypsych.org).

I'll admit to you right now that the way I experience energy most strongly is kinesthetic. That means I feel it in my body. I feel things like goose bumps, waves, tightness and looseness. Often, I feel things in my body that aren't part of me but give me messages about how I can serve someone else who needs attention and what kind of pain they're dealing with.

Now that I've had several years to get in tune with what energy is and how my system is kinesthetic, when I begin to feel someone else's pain it doesn't scare me anymore. I no longer feel uncertain about my ability to send and receive energy because I know it happens. I can reliably trust my gift of energy awareness.

Perhaps you have a gift in a different form. If you are visual, you may see energy around things or people. You might see images or have pictures flow into your mind offering information and insight about the energy around the situation. Trust that. Listen. Feel. Hear. See. Touch. Taste. Allow energy to speak to you in the way you love to receive it. Don't put limits on this. Simply allow it to happen.

Your Thoughts and Intentions

"The more you lose yourself in something bigger than yourself, the more energy you will have."
Norman Vincent Peale

Energy flows where intention goes. Energy also flows where attention goes. Thoughts, beliefs and focused intentions are energy. We create all sorts of powerful things in our mind. You might have heard of the law of attraction, which basically says that like attracts like. In our minds if we create feelings and thoughts that represent what we want or desire, and allow ourselves to feel those things, we create a powerful electromagnetic field, starting to put the wheels in motion to attract those experiences and desires to manifest in the physical form.

I've personally seen this happen over and over again, yet continue to find it somewhat hard to believe. It doesn't make sense to the part of me who has an MBA and a chemistry science degree that somehow there is a law of nature that makes physical things manifest from non-physical thoughts. And yet, I know that to be true.

The important thing to remember is that when you put attention to something, you're putting energy there. Be careful what you put your attention to, especially when you've got a choice between a positive and a negative place to put your attention. The more you reframe your attention on the positive side of things, the more positive experiences and positive situations you're going to attract.

Negative Thoughts Are Inspiration

It's okay to catch yourself in the moment with a negative thought. I always tell my clients that a negative thought is simply an inspiration for a positive thought. Don't deny that you're having the negative thought. See it, accept the truth within the thought and try to figure out what the exact opposite of that thought is. Put your attention there instead. Accept that you're having a negative thought and move your attention to the positive thought. Remember, and I'll repeat this again, *energy flows where intention or attention goes*. Mind your mind, be careful where you put it, and keep it positive.

You Already Know what Energy Imbalance Feels Like

Isn't it funny that when all is well, life is flowing and everything's very comfortable, we barely take notice at all? On the other hand, there are very clear symptoms of energy imbalance. They help get our attention. They do it well almost every time. Some of the symptoms can include brain fog, lack of coordination, frustration, difficulty concentrating, confusion, overwhelmedness, disorganization and even scattered thinking.

If you find yourself feeling those symptoms of imbalance, it's time to pay attention and become aware of what you might be able to do to take better care of your energy. I will give you many ideas throughout this book, but keep in mind that balanced, flowing energy can be overlooked because it feels so good. When you're having trouble, that's a reminder to tune in, pause and get back into the flow for balance.

One of the quickest ways to balance your energy is the deep, full breath. So before I teach you any other techniques, remember the deep, full breath. Take a full breath right now, and then continue reading.

When More than One Are Gathered

"For where two or three gather in my name, there am I with them."
The Bible, Matthew 18:20. New International Version, 2011

There is something about the energy of groups that is fascinating and quite powerful. Jesus spoke of this and you've probably also observed it, too. When many people get together there is an amplification of energy, especially when they're all cooperating or working on something together.

It wasn't until I began doing workshops teaching Emotional Freedom Techniques (EFT) and coaching in group settings that I understood this in a new way. I always invited my audience members to tap their own EFT treatment points as I worked with a volunteer on stage. It made sense that the experience would help them learn the treatment sequence and also what it felt like for them personally. The founder of Emotional Freedom Techniques, Gary Craig, whom I have studied with personally, had always recommended group participation as part of his way of teaching EFT, referring to it as "borrowing benefits."

It soon became apparent to me that the healing results in group settings were often far more exquisite than what I might expect from individual work. Not only was the person whom I was working with finding true relief from some deep pain, but the majority of audience members were reporting some amazing emotional shifts and healing experiences. They reported feeling wonderful even though I wasn't focusing the treatment on them. By simply tapping together, far more people could be helped in a single hour. That caught my attention.

I always appreciate the power that groups can send into a healing situation. When thoughts and intentions are pointed in a similar direction, miraculous things happen. Group support brings even more energy to a situation. Know that when more than one gathers, that healing capacity is multiplied and amplified.

Healthy Energy Habits

Putting energy awareness and energy balance practices into daily life is simple. Energy self-care is healthy and delivers immediate benefits. With as little as five minutes each day devoted to energy self-care, you will begin to notice more focus, clarity, productivity and a sense of greater well-being. I have found the daily energy routines included within Donna Eden's books, *Energy Medicine* and *Energy Medicine for Women*, to be among the best out there. Donna Eden's "Five Minute Energy Routine" is particularly worth mentioning and given in brief below. For the full explanation, I suggest you purchase her books and attend her workshops because they are outstanding.

If you enjoy a challenge and have 5 minutes to spare, you might also want to try the Five Tibetan Fountain of Youth Exercises* each morning immediately upon waking. These are five Tibetan exercises that are much like yoga. When performed daily, I have noticed increased energy, flexibility, optimal core muscle tone and better memory. These exercises are difficult and should be done gradually and with permission from your physician if you are not currently involved in regular exercise.

You will learn more about the Five Tibetan Exercises in Chapter 2. The key is to choose an energy care routine that you enjoy and commit to do for three or more weeks. Many experts agree that three to four weeks of consistent practice is needed to truly activate a new habit.

Donna Eden's Five Minute Awakening Routine**

Upon waking, (before leaving the bedroom is best) do the following to raise, harmonize and amp up your energy for the day. Have a 16 ounce glass of water before you begin. Refer to Figure 1 for location of points mentioned in the routine.

---

* Ancient Secrets of the Fountain of Youth by Peter Kelder. Doubleday, 1998.

** Summarized from pages 51-62 of *Energy Medicine for Women* Copyright 2008 by Donna Eden and David Feinstein PhD

Learn more at www.innersource.net

The Triple Thump (30 Seconds)

For general health, wellness and immune system support, tap each of these points with your fingertips or a loose fists 7 to 10 times. Breathe deeply as you tap. Repeat steps 1 through 3 three times:

1. Both left and right K-27 points (slightly below the collarbone)

2. Thymus point (bony plate at the center of the chest)

3. Liver LV-14 points (under breast)

AM Cross Crawl (30 seconds)

This routine connects the energy across your body and corrects homolaterality (energy not crossing the body correctly):

- Stand and touch your left hand to your right knee, lifting the knee up to facilitate the connection.

- Touch your right hand to your left knee.

- Continue with left hand to right knee and so on. Advanced users can touch their elbows to knees. Repeat 12 or more times.

The Wayne Cook Posture (90 seconds for both sides)
- Sit with a straight spine

- Place your right foot over your left knee

- Wrap your left hand around your right ankle

- Cover the ball of the left foot, with the palm of the right hand, curling fingers around the "little toe side" of the foot

- Breathe in slowly as you pull the right leg toward you.

- Reverse legs and repeat – crossing left foot over right knee.

Forehead and Crown Pulls (30 seconds)

Place fingertips of both hands at the center of your forehead, over the eyebrows. Putting pressure on the forehead, pull your hands apart until they reach the hairline. Move the fingertips to the center of the crown of the head, press lightly on the scalp as you pull the fingers apart. Move fingertips to the back of the head and repeat. Place fingertips on the lowest part of the back of the head, pressing as you repeat the sequence. Repeat the sequence moving down the neck. Finish by resting your fingertips over each shoulder and pulling them forward, over the top of each shoulder as you breathe deeply.

Lymph Massage (30–60 seconds)

This is a great one to do in the shower. Gently massage the tender points or "sore spots" on each side of the upper chest/breast. You can also massage the points on either side of the midline from the sternum to the navel. Finish by massaging along the lower edge of the ribs and rib cage.

Make sure to notice and document the changes you observe as you implement new ways to care for your energetic health. One of the best things to do as you start a new habit is to rate your current energetic state. I like to use a simple scale of zero to 10. Ten being a high, positive state. Zero being the lowest state. Think of it like the fuel gauge on your car: 10 is full and 0 is empty.

If you're feeling invigorated, enthusiastic and passionate and ready to tackle just about anything, of course you're probably close to a 10. We've all had those days where we just don't feel like we're in the flow of anything. We're physically tired, mentally foggy, or emotionally drained. That might be a zero or a one, a good time to take a break, a nap or perhaps even a vacation to get powered up again.

In the appendix section at the end of this book, you will find an assessment tool that will help you assess your energy makeover status and a grid for tracking your daily self-estimated energy level. Becoming more aware of your present energetic state will allow you to master and maintain optimal, balanced and flowing energy. By regularly assessing your energy, you will also develop a better sense of when you're depleted, so that you don't get so low that you've got to take yourself out of the game.

Energy as We Age

If you've recently been in charge of caring for a toddler, you know that there are no bounds to the energy of youth. Those little people have stamina, attention, physical vigor and loud voices, too. Toddlers are actively engaging in their world with every sense, and with an intensity that is astounding. It's natural to hope and pray that you'll

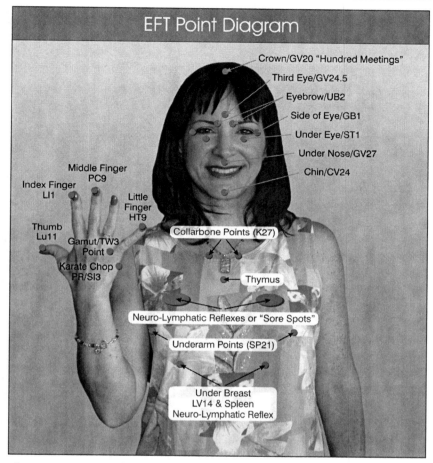

Figure 1 - EFT and Self-Care Treatment Point Diagram

hold onto your own physical stamina, mental clarity, intelligence, voice and astounding abilities well past your 90th birthday, right?

What happens to our energy as we age? Unfortunately when you think of most elderly people and their relative energetic state, it probably makes you nervous, doesn't it? Can aging be postponed or delayed? My answer to this is YES as well. Of course we have physical bodies and, of course, those bodies will change over the years. But, energy flows through those bodies. Balanced energy allows the organs and the physical systems within our bodies to stay in a more optimal form.

Eastern medicine has known about energy as a youth preservation tool for thousands of years. I didn't pick up on this connection personally until I started practicing EFT, a simple self-care technique that involves tapping on energy meridian endpoints to balance energy in the body, release negative emotions and connect with more positive thoughts, feelings and energy flows.

If you're new to energy, here are a few key terms that are part of the human energy system:

Meridians: These are energetic pathways or highways within the body. Just as the heart pumps blood throughout the body, the meridian system distributes life force energy to every organ. Meridians also help to regulate metabolic functions, detoxification and the formation of healthy new cells. In order for your immune, nervous, endocrine, circulatory, respiratory, digestive, skeletal, muscular, and lymphatic systems to be healthy, meridian flow is essential. There are 14 major meridians that move energy through your body. When meridians become blocked, the decrease of energy flow to vital organs can result in "dis-ease." Acupuncture is a healing method that accesses specific electromagnetically charged points along these meridians. When these acupoints are stimulated with needles, physical pressure or tapping on the skin's surface, energy can be balanced and redistributed along the meridian pathway.

Chakras: A variety of ancient Indian texts make reference to seven main energy centers or vortices that align with the spinal column and control the inflow and outflow of universal life force energy or qi. The word chakra in Sanskrit translates to "wheel" in reference to these swirling centers of energy. Each of the seven chakras is located in relationship to both a major nerve plexus and a major gland within the endocrine system. Western medical technology is just beginning to validate and measure that chakras possess a vibrational frequency that can be measured on the skin above each chakra point.

While meridian pathways deliver energy to the organs, the chakras differ in that they surround the organs with energies and may act like energy transformers, stepping down energy from one frequency to another. Each chakra connects to a specific part of human awareness including survival, creativity, identity, love, expression, intuition and spiritual connection to Source. There is good reason to take chakras seriously: ancient Indian wisdom taught that every significant life event is encoded within the chakra energy. Additional information about the 7 chakras may be found in Chapter 6.

Biofield: The biofield refers to the energy that extends through and beyond the physical body. Some sensitive individuals are able to see the biofield, and claim to have witnessed colors, layers, images and movement within it. For most of us, the concept of biofield can be thought of as our invisible energy field that may pull in tightly around us at times, yet also has the capacity to expand far beyond our physical bodies. Thoughts, emotions and intention can all be part of the information contained and transmitted through the biofield. If you consider yourself intuitive or are someone who prays for the benefit of others, both are examples of how you have used your biofield to receive and send information. Modern equipment is able to confirm that subtle energy emission exists beyond the body through the use of SQUID and other electromagnetically sensitive devices.

Unlimited Potential for Regular People

Is it really possible for ordinary folks like you and me to build energy, feel great and stay healthy, even as we age, by working with our natural human energy? Of course it is. We are so lucky to be living in a time when an abundance of energy boosting methods are readily available for self-care. Effective practices such as qi gong, tai chi, reiki, and acupuncture can trace their roots to the emperors in the Far East who hired masters of their time to study the secrets to the fountain of youth: physical stamina, influential power, sexual prowess and, of course, eternal life. These leaders never wanted to give up their thrones or their power, so energy-building methods made perfect sense to them.

Although the ancient masters created herbal remedies and interventions that worked wonders for the emperors, these solutions were rarely shared with the common folk until much more recently. With the dawn of the internet, modern medicine, the information age and just plain common sense, regular folks like you and me can now explore abundant options for energetic health, youth and wholeness from both ancient wisdom and modern discovery.

There's plenty of energy to go around. All you need to do is decide that you want more.

Experiences Awaken Energy Awareness

It may seem odd that I had been managing the marketing program for a clinic specializing in the integration of energy therapies with conventional medicine for over a year, yet didn't begin to understand how energy really worked until I attended that conference in Switzerland. After returning from that meeting in 2001, I started following the EFT meridian self-care tapping methods by tapping on some specific points on my body. I also began trying some of Donna Eden's energy routines. Just about every energy intervention made me feel great. Furthermore, years later as I used EFT and energy self-care practices in sessions with clients, beyond my own self-care, my health kept getting better and better. Soon I had more techniques and tools I was using regularly as part of my daily care including yoga, affirmations, chakra balancing, breath work and meditation.

I can honestly say that at 52 years of age, I am feeling better and clearer than I have for most of the last 30 years. I attribute this to energy awareness and balance. Yes, I do have some pretty good habits and I have made good choices. Working consciously with my energy system has allowed me to take on better habits and new challenges, and to master those challenges with ease. It's been a delightful surprise.

You too can find a way to build balance and optimize your energy. This book will give you plenty of ideas. Get in touch with what it feels like to work with your own energy system through the exercises in each chapter. Keep track of how your Energy Makeover® is working for you. Notice your resilience, especially during turbulent times. Celebrate and be grateful. Simply being aware of your energetic state is the way to improve it.

You need not study with a master for years to get results. You can begin now. You can do it in a way that fulfills your unique set of physical, emotional and intellectual needs without really having to make much fuss about it. At the end of each chapter of Energy Makeover®, a section called "Practice Time" will offer you exercises you can use to recognize energy in more ways than you thought possible. You will soon have an individualized approach you can apply to your daily life.

Expect this to be easier than you thought it would be. In fact, you may realize that you're already doing some positive things that are good for your energy. If that's the case, this book will simply reinforce the great habits you already have in place.

Practice Time

1. Think about your unique bandwidth and the signals you send. What five words best describe the authentic YOU? Who are you in terms of your energetic message and the values you hold dear?

2. Which of your energetic senses are most sensitive? Which sense is already working really well to get your attention on a regular basis? Jot down a few notes about how you experience each of these senses as energy.

   a. Sight

   b. Hearing

   c. Feeling/touch

   d. Taste

   e. Smell

3. Use three adjectives to describe how you experience a lack of energy balance. What unpleasant physical and emotional sensations regularly get your attention?

4. Think of a day when everything felt like it was running perfectly, in good orderly flow. What three words best describe how you felt in that optimal situation? Note: If you haven't had a good day recently, jot down three words that are the opposite of what you posted in number three above.

5. Try the "Five Minute Routine" mentioned on pages 24 - 26.

6. Determine your need for an Energy Makeover® using the Self-Assessment in Appendix I. Use the daily tracking grid in Appendix II to keep track of your energy status for the next 90 days. What do you notice? What are you more aware of when it comes to your unique energy system?

Chapter 2

Get Back Into Your Body

"The body never lies."
Martha Graham

"Take care of your body. It's the only place you have to live."
Jim Rohn

The Gift

You were born with an amazing gift: a wonderful creation that is able to both transmit and receive energy. It's your body. Maybe you've spent most of your life oblivious to this fact, just as I did. Our bodies and our senses are the interface that both gives us a separate self while allowing us to interact with one another and our environment. We hear, taste, feel, touch and smell the world around us with this body. We get around. We have fun. We sleep. We do all sorts of things.

Likewise, our bodies allow us to be heard, smelled, touched, seen, and even tasted once in a while as we go about our lives.

Pain

Sometimes if we're surrounded by all the technology and gadgets that exist to make life easier, we almost forget that we have a physical body. It isn't until pain rises up and calls for attention that we really remember we are physical creatures, too.

Have you ever let your life get so out of balance that you suddenly found yourself incapacitated by illness or intense pain, to the extent that you had to completely stop? Isn't it funny how the body cries for attention but we'll go out of our way to ignore it day upon day? Sometimes we must endure several painful episodes because we choose to act like we don't have bodies, and we keep trudging away in spite of all the warnings. When we ignore our bodies there will be consequences. Eventually our body will make life so miserable that we must wake up and pay attention to it.

Allow me to help you get more in touch with your body right now. Follow these steps:

1. Close your eyes. Put your feet flat on the ground and take a few nice full breaths.

2. Check in with your body. Begin at your head and scan down, noticing where you are experiencing tightness, tension, discomfort or restricted movement. What does your breath feel like? Is it easy to breathe? Do you notice tension or a tight feeling in your chest or lungs? Jot down the location of your discomfort and then note the relative distress on a scale of zero to 10.

3. Ask yourself whether what you are discovering is new or if this is something you've been dealing with over a longer period of time? Do you know when this began? Is there a specific cause or event you can tie to it?

4. Ask yourself if anything you are feeling is connected to an emotion. What would that emotion be? If there was a story or lesson this feeling of discomfort was trying to communicate to you, what would that message be? Be curious and see what comes to mind. Now, open your eyes and jot down a few notes about this experience.

Maybe you're one of the lucky people who didn't find any pain or discomfort when you did that quick scan and got in touch with your body. Bravo for you! That means you've got something great to pay attention to. Your body's working! Don't think you missed something by not having pain. That's a sign that your energy probably is flowing pretty well, so pat yourself on the back. Pay more attention to how comfortable your body is these days because what you put your thoughts to, expands. As mentioned in the last chapter, where your attention goes, there's energy. When you notice good things you can amplify and attract more good things.

Exercise Balances Energy

Aging is one of those blessings that help even the most oblivious person realize they really do have a body. The wisest people awaken to the fact that now is the time to take better care of it.

I spent over two decades of my adult life running around like a chicken with her head cut off, living from one frantic moment to the next. I was out of breath most of the day until I crashed into bed each night. Yes, I seemed to get a whole lot accomplished, but it was not very enjoyable, meaningful or fun.

A reliable source of energy-boosting balance throughout my life, and even during those frantic times, has always been movement. Whether it was running, dancing, brisk walking or calisthenics, I could usually count on physical activity to rejuvenate me, make me feel better, and help me shake off stress. Even during those most stressed out years of my life, I was lucky enough to have a gym in my workplace where I could escape for a good sweat and a nice escape for activity in the middle of my day.

It was amazing that just moving my feet and arms vigorously for 30 minutes or so could restore mental clarity and a good mood simultaneously. Now I also know that I was feeding my energy system exactly what it needed by alternating the activation of my right and left brain as I was breathing deeply and having my feet fully connected to the ground. During exercise those movements were helping to balance my energy. I didn't even realize it at the time. All I knew is that it felt good and that it was enough to keep me engaged in that habit.

Exercise is a habit I still adhere to today because it makes me feel so well. It makes sense for a person who experiences energy in a kinesthetic way through feeling physical sensations. Maybe you're like me. If you really love exercising, pay attention to the ways you feel energy through your body.

Searching for the Fountain of Youth

As my 40th birthday passed, I started to notice that my stamina was really fading. What used to be easy was feeling heavier. I would awaken with a few more aches and pains each morning, especially after my workouts. I was starting to gain a few extra pounds, too. As I looked in the mirror each morning I was not sure I recognized that tired, older woman looking back at me. I didn't like what I saw. Fortunately I started looking for answers.

At that time I was working as a business development director for a group medical practice specializing in integrative medicine and preventative health. I had access to a load of resources, and practitioners who understood both health and energy balance.

One day I was assigned to research some of the most successful natural health books, and stumbled upon one titled *The Ancient Secrets of the Fountain of Youth* by Peter Kelder. I was intrigued. I brought the book to the attention of Sherri Tenpenny, DO, our medical director, and asked if I could purchase the book for our practice. As a bestseller, I hoped this book could guide Dr. Sherri with the book she was developing for her patients. I wanted to understand the formula that made this book was so successful. Deep inside I knew—it offered both hope and a simple process. Nobody wants to grow older. Everyone wants the secret of the fountain of youth. I, too, was curious about what was in that book.

Once I secured a copy of the book, I was pleased to find that it was small and relatively short. I opened the book, and to my delight not only was it a book of information, but it had simple pictures. The book explained five exercises that you could do daily to restore balance and healthy energy flow in your body.

The book claimed that the exercises worked by invigorating the body's endocrine system. The endocrine system is the part of our body that manages our hormones and stress response. The endocrine system is closely linked to every bodily function.

I was already exercising, so a book with five little exercises that could be done in less than five minutes was attractive. It was something that I could commit to do. I read the book and quickly learned there was caution involved. You were not supposed to do the full set of exercises right from the beginning. Even somebody like me, who was very fit, was advised to only do three reps of each exercise the first week, gradually building to 21 reps of each exercise by the end of seven or more weeks.

Soon I was actually doing the exercises and they were fun. Some were more challenging for me than others. I developed a favorite right away: #5. The Five Tibetans became a new habit for me. I did them deliberately and religiously every day upon waking, just as the book said. They helped me feel *really great*.

Now here's where it got interesting. Once I had advanced to the full 21 reps of each exercise every day, I started noticing some interesting new things. I became more connected to the present moment than ever before. I also noticed that I was picking up on things that I couldn't see or hear, but I knew. It was like I was being given information, but I didn't know who was giving it to me. I was receiving vivid dreams at night that were helping me work out problems.

I was also receiving information from somebody on the other side. I suspected this somebody was my husband's sister who had passed away just a few short months before of a tragic illness. She was only in her forties.

I wondered, "What have I done? What have I activated by doing these exercises that has caused this flow of information to me, sometimes making me think I was a little bit crazy?" The information I was receiving was good, loving information. It was helpful. It was creating ways for me to get through my day more intuitively, in better connection with the people around me. I also experienced physical comfort because the exercises were really helping my body. I was more flexible, toned and had better core strength. My spine felt great. I was hooked.

I tell you all of this today because I began these exercises over 10 years ago. I've been doing those exercises every single day, and I truly believe that there's something magical about them, although I don't fully understand it. If you get the book you'll find that each exercise is attributed to certain parts of the energy system and certain organs and glands. For the best description of the exercises and their benefits, get a copy of *The Ancient Secrets of The Fountain of Youth* by Peter Kelder.

If you are curious about the Five Tibetan Exercises, you can see a short video demonstration at www.energymakeover4U.com. Refer to Figure 2 for a brief overview of the exercises.

I highly recommend that you buy the book itself because there are so many details within the book about the exercises and the history

Betsy's Energy Makeover Recommends
The 5 Tibetan "Fountain of Youth" Exercises

Source: Kelder, Peter *The Ancient Secret of the Fountain of Youth Book 2* Doubleday 1998

Note: Please seek your doctor's advice before engaging in exercise. These are difficult and you are urged to start slowly, gradually starting with 3 reps the first week, building to the suggested 21 repetitions per day by week 7.

Rite #1 Clockwise Spinning "T"

Benefits circulation, varicose veins, osteoporosis, flow of cerebral-spinal fluid, prevention of headaches and mental clarity. Powerful exercise that increases the spin of all of the energy centers.

You may be amazed how the energy from these exercises attracts pets.

Rite #2 Leg Raises

Benefits thyroid, adrenals, kidneys, digestive system, sexual organs. Helps with irregular period and menopause. Strengthens abdomen, legs and arms. Chakras 5,3,2, and 1.

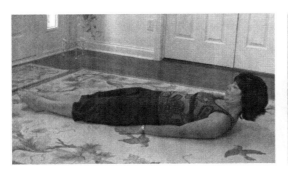

38

Rite #3 Kneeling Back Bend

Benefits arthritis, meno-
pause/menstrual symp-
toms, digestion, back
and neck pain, sinus
congestion. Chakras 5,
3 and 2.

Rite #4 The Table

Benefits arthritis, osteoporosis, menstrual/menopause symptoms,
sinus congestion and immune system. Chakras 5,4,3,2, and 1.

Rite #5 Upward Dog/Downward Dog

Benefits back pain, leg and neck stiffness, thyroid function, sexual
organs, digestive and bowel function, immune system and clears
sinuses.

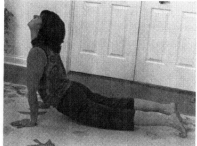

of the exercises. Why they came to the attention of the author and some of the ways they work with the body.

The reason I was intrigued by the book (beyond the title itself) was the story it contained about Colonel Bradford, an English Army officer who had the opportunity to go to the far corners of Tibet and learn these exercises as taught by the monks at the monastery. When he returned from his travels, people who knew him before he left were astonished to see that he stood straight; his hair had turned dark, with barely a touch of any gray. He was lean, healthy and full of stamina. What Colonel Bradford had learned from these Tibetans was that these exercises activated the body's seven energy centers, which in English are typically called vortices. The Hindus refer to them as chakras. You can't see them but they are very real energy fields. These seven energy centers govern the seven glands in the body's endocrine system which includes the thyroid, pituitary, pineal, reproductive organs and adrenal glands. These are the regulators of the body's functions, including the aging process.

The five exercises may not be for everyone but I encourage you to learn about them. Perhaps there are other exercises that you could incorporate to increase your well-being and allow you to become more in touch with your body. Yoga is another practice that I highly recommend and find quite complementary to the practice of the Five Tibetan Rites. Find something that you can do to help remind you that you are a physical being, whether it's a simple exercise program, breathing with awareness, taking walks or doing some sort of physical activity.

Mindfully become a physical creature and you will soon discover the benefits that are possible by acknowledging and fully occupying your body.

Breathing is Energy

There are so many ways to boost energy, I can't help but be excited for you, and for me. However, if I was challenged to name the single most powerful thing a human being could do to bring the most immediate improvement to health and energy balance, my vote would go to breathing. The kind that is slow, full and rhythmic. Throughout this book I'll teach you a number of techniques for working with your energy that may look funny if you do them in public. Breathing in public, however, will never embarrass you—another reason breathing is my number one. Breathing is something you can do anywhere. If you didn't do it you would die. Unfortunately we cheat ourselves by letting stress reduce our breaths to short, shallow wisps of nothing. Breath is energy. If you want to stay young and fully present, just breathe. Breathing brings oxygen to your brain for mental clarity. Breathing brings your attention back into your body. Breathing increases your metabolism so that you can burn up to 30 percent more calories per hour. Breathing sends healing oxygen to your organs and to every cell, helping you repair and regenerate. Breathing slowly tricks your parasympathetic nervous system into thinking that there is nothing to be worried about, and triggers your heart to beat in a coherent and healing rhythm. How nice is that? When in doubt, take a nice big, full breath. If you are really stressed, close your eyes when you breathe. If you are interested in trying a very powerful form of breathing, try some belly breathing. Here's how:

1. Put your hand on your belly right by your belly button.

2. Push your belly out against your hand as you inhale.

3. With your hand on your belly pull your navel to your spine as you exhale.

Belly breathing is a great way to relieve the stress in your head and to move your energy down into your center so that it is aligned with your heart. For a video demonstration of this belly breathing technique, go to www.energymakeover4U.com

Water: The Lubricant for Your Energy System

Did you know that over 70 percent of your body is water? In fact, water makes up 80 percent of your blood, 80 percent of your brain and 75 percent of your muscles. Water cushions your joints and your organs. One of my favorite natural health experts, Dr. Joseph Mercola, is quoted as saying, "For the average American, the single most important physical step they could take to improve their health would be to switch all of their fluids over to pure drinking water."

Dr. Masaru Emoto, an internationally recognized researcher, has determined that thoughts can have a powerful effect on the way ice crystals form in water. Using high speed photography, Dr. Emoto has shown that water, which makes up so much of our planet and our bodies, can be healed and transformed through thoughts of love and gratitude. This research holds hope and positive implications for the future of our environment and the well-being of every life form on this planet. Saying kind words or a prayer over your next drink of water is highly recommended.

We live in a world made up of huge quantities of water. Our bodies are water and we need constant hydration in order to thrive. Water within our bodies carries electromagnetic energy and frequency. I often refer to water as the lubricant for the body's energy system. If you want an Energy Makeover®, you must drink water. There's no getting around it. Water is part of the signaling system we are all born with. If you want optimal energy balance, you need to be hydrated and you need to stay hydrated.

Water allows our bodies to eliminate waste and toxins and help us look good by giving us moist skin, thinner middles and bright, sparkly eyes. Water helps balance the pH in our blood. Water helps us keep mental focus, optimal concentration. Don't expect to look young, stay healthy, have fun, experience high energy or get anything done without keeping yourself in touch with a constant supply of pure water.

Wake Up to Water

One of the things I always recommend is water first thing in the morning. Think about it. You've been asleep for seven to nine hours. It makes sense that you might be dehydrated. Start your day, before you do anything else, with two cups (16 ounces) of purified water. Drink this water before you have that coffee or tea in the morning. Then continue to drink more water throughout the day. If you're a 130 pound woman, you probably should be drinking about eight cups of water a day. If you're a man, 10 might be a better number. A good rule of thumb is for every pound you weigh, divide that by two. If you weigh 200 pounds, divide 200 in half, which is 100 ounces, or approximately 12 cups.

Keep in mind that it really is important to remain hydrated. A mere two percent drop in the body's water volume can bring on dizziness, muscle cramps, fatigue and problems with concentration. Just a slight change in your hydration can bring about fatigue, lower productivity, brain fog and other symptoms that we may think are symptoms of aging. It's not! It's our need for water. As you begin adding more water, especially first thing in the morning, pay attention to how you feel.

Save your health and the planet. Don't use those plastic bottles of water. Get some reusable stainless steel or glass containers for your water. And take those containers of water with you wherever you go, whether it's to your desk, in your car or wherever.

I highly recommend a water filtration system so that you have an abundant supply of purified water. I use the Nikken PiMag Home Filtration System. This is an alkaline water system that also removes toxins such as chlorine, while adding back essential minerals to balance your health. Alkaline water can help counteract acidity in the body which may help to reduce inflammation. There are other water purification solutions out there that may work just as well for you. Find one you love and drink to your health.

Food Equals Energy, Too

Just as water and air are an essential part of your energy balance, food is, too. You've already been told what not to eat so I won't do anything more to make you feel guilty about your diet. The best foods, as you know, are the ones that are minimally processed, natural, fresh and preferably grown locally. Look to fill yourself up with fresh fruits, vegetables, whole grains and lean sources of protein. Pay attention to which foods make you feel better, and especially to those foods that help you feel your best.

Pay particular attention to the foods that are easy on your digestive system. Food sensitivities may get worse as you age, so use your intuition to guide healthy and comfortable decisions for your personal diet.

As a lifetime member of Weight Watchers® since 1991, I personally endorse their PointsPlus program. If you need guidelines for healthy, balanced eating, Weight Watchers® is a great place to start. It's hands down one of the most complete, reasonably priced, nutritionally balanced systems for establishing a healthy eating plan. You can find online resources or a local meeting at www.weightwatchers.com

Food and Depression

Did you know that some foods have been linked to depression? I was astonished to find out fish oil is a very valuable nutritional supplement and eating fish can help reduce or eliminate post-partum depression. Fish oil is also associated with helping people maintain highly positive moods and with reducing inflammation as well as the painful symptoms caused by inflammation. If you're not currently taking fish oil supplements or eating fish on a regular basis, this might be something to try as part of your Energy Makeover®.

The *British Journal of Psychiatry* recently reported that regular consumption of fish, fruits, vegetables and low fat meats correlated with lower incidences of depression. The same study found that eating processed meats, sweet desserts, processed foods, fast foods, fried foods and foods high in dairy fat provoked depression symptoms.

Enjoy Your Chocolate!

One food that you might want to have more of is chocolate. I personally eat a little square of deep, dark chocolate every single day, even when I'm traveling. I never feel guilty about it. Chocolate contains powerful antioxidants called polyphenols, which help keep you healthy by fighting off free radicals, highly reactive compounds that can cause cellular damage. A recent study found that people who indulged once a week in chocolate had a 22 percent lower risk of stroke than those who didn't eat any chocolate. I can't imagine not eating any chocolate! The study went further to note that dark chocolate is always the best choice for health and prevention.

Your Heart as an Energy Center

Did you know that your heart is central to your body's energy system? Your heart is an intelligent guide to help you fully live in your body. Your heart is faster than your brain in sending vibration and subtle signals throughout your body. Your heart chakra is the middle of your seven chakras and can be viewed as the center where earth and God meet within you. Your heart sends the biggest and most intense signals out from your body—a signal so strong that instruments can now detect it many feet away from you.

According to nearly two decades of research by the Institute of HeartMath, people around you are subtly aware of your heart rhythm and will synchronize their heart rhythms to yours when the moment is right. HeartMath developed a monitoring system to help people train and understand how to mindfully control their heart rate variability, and by doing so promote health and a greater sense of well-being.

When I became aware of HeartMath research several years ago, I purchased their emWave personal heart rate variability monitor for my coaching practice. It is a monitoring tool I realized could help my clients develop a greater ability to connect, relax and take control of their bodies as vehicles for being present and healthy in daily life. The HeartMath heart variability monitor teaches a client to achieve and hold heart coherence in real time. Coherence is a state of balance between the brain and the heart. When the heart rate is in that coherent, orderly state, the body produces pleasant neurotransmitters, the blood pressure naturally lowers, and the body destroys harmful free radicals. Perhaps the greatest benefit comes from the personal peace that accompanies this coherent state. People can learn to manage their stress better, which in turn helps them to age more gracefully.

The beauty of the HeartMath monitor is that you can see how you're doing in the present moment on a small handheld device or laptop computer. I was astounded during my very first session to see how my thoughts and my breath had an impact on my heart. I quickly and easily learned to manage my heart rate variability simply by setting my intention. The people at the HeartMath Institute, who have been studying this for almost twenty years, have found that once a person learns how to manage a coherent heart rate variability status for just four minutes, the body remembers how to return to the coherent state by simply setting an intention. I'm one of those people now. I don't need the machine to know I'm in a coherent state. I simply send myself there and enjoy how good it feels.

I've always been excited to give my clients and experience with the HeartMath monitor so that they can see first-hand how one positive thought can bring them into a strong state of coherence. You can bring your heart into a coherent state with HeartMath's Quick Coherence Technique using three simple steps:

1. Breathe. We already covered that earlier in this chapter. Breathe fully and deeply.

2. Focus your attention on your heart. Often that means closing your eyes so you can get out of your head, so you can really be in your heart.

3. Hold a thought of gratitude or appreciation. Think of something you love.

Doing these three steps simultaneously will help the heart rhythm naturally achieve a coherent, regular, balanced pattern.

Remember, you hold the key in your heart. The heart is powerful. You can engage the practice of heart coherence for better sleep, naturally lift your mood, heal grief, enhance athletic performance, attract a more purposeful life, transform relationships and be more productive. Learn more about HeartMath at www.HeartMath.com.

Your Body and the Earth Connection

As creatures who live amidst the trappings of indoor environments and modern society, we can easily lose our connection to nature and the earth. Days and even weeks can pass between those times when we get off the cement and out on the grass, beach, ocean, woods or fields that our ancestors were so naturally connected to.

What a pity it is that as time away from nature stretches we are robbed of our natural ability to thrive. It's easy to reconnect with the earth, and you may notice a greater sense of well-being if you take just a few moments to do it more regularly. Here are just a few ways to connect with the earth:

- Take a walk outside amidst trees and nature, even if walking on cement. Research has shown that just exposing yourself to some of the trace chemicals that trees put into the air around you can lift your spirit. So why not get this natural dose of an anti-depressant?

- Lie on the ground under a tree. Always a nice idea, especially in the summertime.

- Walk barefoot. Have your feet on the floor or the ground more often than not.

- Exercise outdoors. Walk, run, skip, walk your dog, get outside, shovel snow if it's that time of year. Get outside.

- Mow the grass, work in your garden, plant something, and harvest something. Do something outside to improve the way your immediate environment looks, but enjoy your time as you connect with the soil, the plants and the living life in your surroundings.

- Sit outdoors in a place that offers a view of natural surroundings. If you can't physically sit outside, position yourself by a window so you can see life around you. Notice the birds in the trees, squirrels and chipmunks running along the ground, and people walking by. While you're at it, get a bird feeder and put it by your favorite window so you have plenty of nature to observe and appreciate throughout the year.

- Add natural scenes to your home, your workplace and your life through artwork and photography. Create nature within your indoor living space.

- Add plants, fresh flowers and silk trees to your décor, especially if you're not good with live plants. Enjoy creating natural environments within the indoors. Bring the outdoors in and enjoy it.

Practice Time

1. Schedule three breathing breaks on your calendar today and the rest of this week. Try the belly breathing technique and notice how it differs from the way you normally breathe. Begin to use breathing as your first defense against stressful moments and challenging situations.

2. Schedule a regular check-up with your physician or nurse practitioner. Determine if there are any health priorities you need to pay particular attention to. Make sure to ask what forms of exercise are safe for you to begin as a daily routine. If you don't have a regular physician, ask your friends for recommendations or visit www.holisticmedicine.org.

3. Drink 16 ounces of water upon waking. Make water your primary beverage of choice. Invest in a great stainless steel water bottle so that you always have an ample supply handy.

4. Try the three-step heart coherence process discussed on page 46 for five minutes. What do you notice?

5. Write in a journal each day about awareness of your physical body. Keep track of your pain, tension, soreness, digestion, breathing and even what seems to be comfortable and working well. Notice what may change from one day to the next.

6. Connect with nature using at least one of the suggestions given on pages 45 - 46. Which one(s) did you choose? Why?

Chapter 3

Let Emotions Be Your Guide

*"Courage is the art of being the only one who knows
you're scared to death."*
Earl Wilson

Like the Rooms of Your House

Emotions are feelings, pleasant or unpleasant, that constantly let us know we are having an energetic intervention with the world around us. Why is it that some people can live most of their lives in a state of pure joy while others can barely muster a smile or a breath of hope?

Growing up, I learned quite a bit by observing the emotional state of my own family members. They gave me good examples of the extremes. My father and his father spent most of their waking hours in states of optimism, hope and joyful connection with the world around them. Being around them was usually very uplifting and enjoyable.

In contrast, many of the women from both sides of my family have a tendency to experience exhaustion, sadness, worry or migraines on a regular and extended basis. My ancestors suffered these symptoms before depression became a common and socially acceptable diagnosis. I remember many times when I felt my energy drain in the presence of these women. It could be both painful and confusing to spend time in their midst during those low points.

I vowed to never let myself get like that, yet I knew the potential was there. The more I read about the growing problem of depression in our society and saw it in my own family and the patients I met during my time managing the group medical practice, I became more passionate about helping others prevent that fall into isolating low emotional states.

If emotions are energy, can they be managed and deliberately brought to a higher place? Even if you have a family history of depression, can you be hopeful about maintaining a positive emotional state throughout your lifespan? My answer to this is a resounding YES, and this is perhaps the most exciting piece of the Energy Makeover®.

Take a moment to consider that emotions are just like the rooms in your house. You may move throughout your house during the day, yet there are a few rooms that are the most familiar and where you spend the most time. Emotions are like those most familiar rooms where we spend the most time. Recognizing where our emotions tend to drift helps us become more aware of our average emotional set point and gives us the power to stay where we are or to choose to move to a better place.

The awareness of your emotional state followed by a deliberate choice or action opens the door to healing. Emotions are a blessing, just as your body and your health are blessings. Emotions give you a place to be. They let you know that you are engaged in life. Feel and honor your emotions because they are the best guideposts to show you the way to something better.

What about Depression?

Depression is like a fast moving river that leads to a treacherous waterfall. Many of us stand on the banks of this river getting pushed closer and closer to the edge. Proactive people recognize the danger early, catch their balance and back away to higher ground. Others are pushed closer and closer to the edge without realizing it as they get lost in daily pressures. The unlucky ones lose their balance, fall in and get swept away.

An astonishing statistic appeared in the February 2008 issue of *Woman's Day*. In a survey of over 6,500 women, 24 percent of respondents indicated that their biggest health concern was depression. That came second only to cancer at 28 percent. It was ahead of diabetes and heart disease. Of course depression is a problem. I have worked with dozens of clients with a history of depression or who struggle on the edge. I have similarly found myself on the edge of depression many times. My family history reminds me that I may be more vulnerable than most.

The real issue, this survey pointed out, is that so many women fear depression. Why does depression fear rank so high? Is it because our society finally acknowledges this struggle publicly? Is it because so many people's lives, including celebrities, are touched by depression in today's complex, stressful world? I suspect it is because depression is so mysterious in the way it attacks and subsides. Adding to that, those who finally get their lives back after an episode of depression forever fear that they'll slip back into the darkness.

How can we remove the fear when depression seems to be winning? It's robbing women of energy and motivation they need to seek help and to recover peaceful lives. Women admit they're exhausted. In that same *Woman's Day* survey, nearly one-third of respondents wished they had more energy.

When I first learned about energy psychology in 2001, I immediately saw great potential for helping people use self-care interventions like Emotional Freedom Techniques to prevent depression, support those who struggle with it and to keep the vulnerable ones balanced and away from the edge. I saw the value of early intervention to teach children and teens how to be more resilient. I recognized how every person could benefit from coaching support and survival tools for those difficult days when life gets tough.

Life balance and self-care are practical common sense, but the formula for each person must be individually tailored. As a coach I'm not in a position to diagnose or treat depression; however I must become part of the solution. The long term life balance solutions offered through coaching and Energy Makeover®, offer so many practical options for self-care. Energy balance can keep people away from the treacherous edge and keep them connected to a long, resilient lifeline for help. I've seen lives change, exhaustion subside and joy return. When fear can be replaced by hope, joyful living prevails.

The Emotional Scale

It has been said that if there were only two emotions, they would be love and fear. If we put them on a scale, love would be the emotion of highest frequency with fear at the opposite end. If you are not certain about your exact emotional state, take a moment to notice if you're isolating yourself from the world around you or connecting to it. High emotional states like love, enthusiasm, joy and bliss are typically those that connect to the outside.

Certainly a variety of specific emotions exist along the emotional scale, and many experts have developed guides and labels to help us identify and raise our emotional states. One of the best emotional scales I've come across is that included by Esther and Jerry Hicks in their excellent book *Ask and It Is Given*. Not only does the book present a framework for understanding the various emotional states in relationship to the extremes of love or fear, but also give each of us permission and perspective for where along the scale find ourselves most easily settling.

The Emotional Scale from *Ask and It Is Given**

1. Love/Joy/Knowledge/Freedom/Appreciation/Empowerment
2. Passion
3. Enthusiasm/Eagerness/Happiness
4. Positive Expectation/Belief
5. Optimism
6. Hopefulness
7. Contentment
8. Boredom
9. Pessimism
10. Frustration/Irritation/Impatience
11. Overwhelm
12. Disappointment
13. Doubt
14. Worry
15. Blame
16. Discouragement
17. Anger
18. Revenge
19. Hatred/Rage
20. Jealousy
21. Insecurity/Guilt/Unworthiness
22. Fear/Grief/Depression/Despair/ Powerlessness

* Jerry & Esther Hicks, Ask and It is Given (Hay House, 2004)
  AbrahamHicks.com

I remember my own wakeup call as I discovered that contentment was situated next to boredom on this scale. Rather than letting myself get upset about boredom, this new awareness allowed me to immediately shift to that higher state of contentment and gain a sense of gratitude. It wasn't so bad to be bored.

My heart aches for those people who live most of their days in those low emotional states of depression, fear, grief and hopelessness. You can't change what you don't know. I impress upon everyone to feel their feelings. Feeling emotions is the door to something better. That's the way it starts. You must feel what you feel and then accept it. Once you've accepted how you feel, then the choice is yours to change it.

Heart Feelings

Take a moment to close your eyes and think of something you absolutely love. Maybe it's a person, a place, a memory, a favorite food or a cherished pet. Whatever it is, just feel this love for a good 60 seconds. As you feel this feeling, ask yourself where in your body do you feel it? My guess is that you feel it right in the center of your chest at your heart. This energy center, the heart, is a powerful one. It is where you feel the love. It is also where you feel the pain of rejection, of grief, of loss. Acknowledge those feelings, especially those in the heart. Feel it and heal it.

The Challenge of Forgiveness

You and I know all too well that hearts can easily be broken, mangled or crushed. It is nearly impossible to get through life without having been rejected, jilted, betrayed or abandoned. How can we possibly maintain high energy emotions when these horrible things are done to us or to our loved ones? How can we possibly move on from the most devastating moments of our lives, especially when the harm was inflicted by somebody who did it deliberately, mindlessly or without bothering to apologize?

It is said that withholding forgiveness is like drinking poison and hoping it will kill the person who did you wrong. Energetically we are letting our energy flow to the person who hurt us, draining our own life force. By holding onto anger, bitterness and hatred, we shift our emotional state to a dangerously low place. It is like slowly bleeding to death.

Unfortunately, even when you know that you should forgive somebody, it is often the hardest thing you will ever do. It feels like you're letting them off the hook. You want them to hurt and to be punished, yet all of that hurt just keeps coming back at you. Forgiveness is a significant energy builder and something to which you should pay attention, even if you aren't ready to fully forgive. Consider opening up a willingness to try.

One of the nicest and simplest energy interventions that we can use for healing and forgiveness is a simple technique called heart massage taught to me by a special teacher, Barbara Stone, PhD. Barbara was my certification consultant when I became a Certified Energy Health Practitioner through the Association for Comprehensive Energy Psychology. I'm not sure Barbara developed this technique but

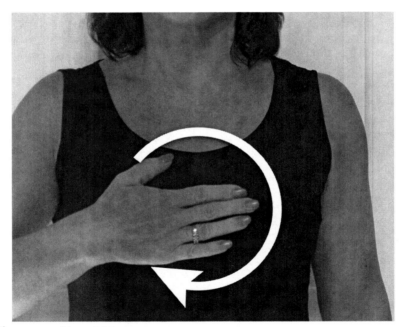

Figure 2 - Heart Massage

it was one that we used many times in sessions together and that she uses often in her teachings. I love it!

To do heart massage, refer to figure 2. Simply hold your open palm of your hand facing your chest, over your heart. Move your hand in a clockwise circle over your heart, as if your chest was the face of a clock. When using your right hand over the heart, you will circle first to the left, then down, right and up. Make that circle without touching your chest, at about 1-2 inches away from your body.

As you continue making the circles over the heart, begin speaking statements that both acknowledge your feelings and set an intention of forgiveness. Allow me to suggest some good example statements you can try as you continue doing the heart massage:

- Even though I am hurting and I feel as though I was deliberately hurt by _____, I deeply and completely honor my feelings and I love and accept myself.

- Even though I am still feeling the pain that has been inflicted upon me by _____, I feel it, I accept it and I love and accept myself fully.

- Even though I've carried this pain so long and I've wanted justice and revenge, I accept these hurtful feelings.

- I accept the darkness that has crept into my awareness and I choose to let it go.

- I release my tormentor.

- I ask for grace to come over me and heal these wounds so that I can step aside and move on.

- I unwind and release the energetic cords that exist between us.

- I allow my tormentor to be free of my hatred, anger and upset.

- I allow the wounds that I've carried to heal now and to reintegrate fully and completely into my energy system.

- I close the breaks in my own system and make them impervious to future attack.

- I build strength through my strength.

- I wish my tormentor peace.

- I send love to anyone else who has felt this kind of pain. I acknowledge all of the broken hearts and I share this healing for their benefit.

- Through the restoration of my wholeness, I have healed all of humanity. As I change, the world changes.

As you finish this exercise and you finish your affirmation statements, place both hands over your heart, one over the other, and breathe. Reverse the hands so that the top hand goes directly on the chest and the other hand moves to the top. Breathe again; allowing yourself to fully integrate the forgiveness work you've done with your heart.

Letting Go of the Nonsense

Are you paying attention to the thoughts going through your head all day? Is that little voice in your head a kind and loving one, who encourages you to keep on going? Or is it a nasty one picking apart every good idea that might come up? Are you listening to and believing this voice? We are what we think and we attract what we think. The beauty of this concept is that we can also choose our thoughts and we can shift our thoughts quickly to better material. You don't have to be stuck listening to that annoying, negative voice.

Let me give you an example. I once had a young comedian I will refer to as Debbie contact me for some help. Debbie had recently had a performance that didn't go so well. Adding to her pain, once she got off the stage she experienced verbal abuse from a fellow comedian. It stung and hurt deeply, especially because this critic was someone she longed to receive a complement from. Instead she was smacked down about as far as she could go.

Those words of criticism stung long after Debbie's performance was over. In fact, that was the nonsense tape playing through her head over and over again for weeks. She'd heard about Emotional Freedom Techniques and how powerful EFT was for helping to let go of negative thoughts, beliefs and unpleasant emotions. We scheduled a session the following week.

As Debbie and I worked together, she was able to access that specific moment in her memory when she heard the words that hurt the most. That was the scene we chose for our first EFT healing intervention. In EFT, we first acknowledge what has happened. I then guided Debbie to accept that it happened and that the incident was over. We tapped on the EFT treatment points as we said the specific phrase that hurt so much.

"You bombed, Deb. We won't be seeing you around here anymore."

Why would we tap on something so negative? You can't change something until you fully engage in it. Although it was briefly painful for Debbie to dwell on the negative words in her memory, she needed to be there energetically to allow the situation to sink in before she could begin to change her response to it.

The beauty of this session was that it took less than five minutes for Debbie to feel, accept, fully own and release all of the negative feelings around those words and that scene. Working on a very specific memory allowed her to really be there emotionally! Tears often come up, signaling a glorious opportunity for transformation. As Debbie's tears subsided, I knew I could begin to shift her to new, positive affirmation statements.

We tapped on these affirmations:

- I am confident and full of joy whenever I am on stage.
- I hear the compliments and feel connection with my audience.
- I can prepare myself for every performance by tapping.
- I am ready to be funny and full of spunk.
- I deserve a standing ovation.

I'm happy to report that the treatment worked. Today, Debbie's both an actress and a comedian. She travels all over the place. She constantly tells me about new opportunities that are coming her way. She liberated herself by forgiving and letting go of negative past experiences. We can no longer say that that negative experience was bad because a huge amount of awareness and growth resulted from it. Because that critic came along, Debbie is now equipped with a tool to help her let go of any kind of nonsense that might arise in the future. She knows how to move on after a set-back. What a blessing.

Remember, even those bad things that happen can serve a greater purpose, and make you stronger. That is the lesson. If you're dealing with any kind of nonsense, remember you can choose to let it go.

Building Confidence behind Closed Doors

When I began working as a personal coach I was astounded by the sadness and the sense of powerlessness people would immediately admit to me once they were behind a closed door. I would never have suspected that these obviously successful and well-balanced people were a mess inside. They were silently tormented by the prominence of their self-doubt and low confidence. Many had endured abuse as children, serious injuries or illness, death of a loved one, abandonment or extreme shame. My eyes have opened much wider to the pain the average person endures over the course of a lifetime. All of us need to stop the negative chatter and seek support in the midst of our own chaos. Remember that you never know what burdens others carry. If you knew, their behavior would make much more sense. It is safe to assume that most people have been wounded. Treat them kindly and tenderly, as you would hope to be treated in your darkest moments.

Sit Up and Smile

Want to know how to get more confidence immediately? Here's something you can do, and it's easy. Researchers at the Ohio State University have found that just sitting upright with a straight spine affects how others see you, as well as how you see yourself and how confident you feel. Want to add some additional power to that? Smile. By simply smiling, you add some good emotions to the situation. That phrase, "Fake it till you feel it," has some truth in it. Sit up straight and smile and you'll even get a little boost in terms of positive neurotransmitters, just by adjusting your body.

Your Voice is an Energy Lifter Too

If sitting up with a smile is not enough for you, add some positive affirmation statements. It's the perfect way to jump start a slow day, or any moment for that matter. Pick a few favorites from this list and say them out loud on a regular basis. Post them in a visible place and share them with somebody who needs a boost. Keep them handy and add to the list as your awareness grows.

It is important to remember that affirmations work best when you say them out loud and with volume and emphasis in your voice. Don't just think them. Shout them.

Here are some of my favorites:

- I know what makes me happy and I attract it deliberately.

- I have the power to bring a smile to someone's face today.

- My favorite song plays in my mind on command.

- My body responds remarkably to all positive suggestions.

- I notice beauty in the small things and I offer gratitude frequently and liberally.

- I am open to expressing love, offering love and accepting love in complete safety.

- I operate freely, with complete integrity, within my own truth.

- I enjoy playing an important role in the Divine plan.

- Each day allows me to open to my greater purpose.

- I comfortably follow subtle signs and intuitive guidance, and experience excellent results.

- When I begin to lose my energy, a simple, full breath completely restores me.

- I am blessed with safety, love, friendship and opportunities.

- I have exactly what I need and I am grateful.

- I am surrounded by a world of beauty, light and meaning.

- I am patient and aware.

- I notice the grace and the Divine in all living creatures.

- I am the answer to someone else's prayer.

Expressing Gratitude

Want an immediate upward emotional shift? Use gratitude as the express train to a more positive emotional state. Being grateful is perhaps one of the most essential elements in sustaining vibrant life, closely following the basics of food, water and sleep. Why is it that we tend to obsess about what isn't perfect in life rather than noticing the things that are going well? We actually have lots to be grateful for, and when we plug into these things, we generate uplifting neurotransmitters in our brain, lower our blood pressure, elevate our mood, and attract more good things into our experience.

Gratitude is a habit that can be strengthened through daily awareness and practice. When you focus on gratitude, you are choosing a very positive thought. When you exercise your gratitude muscles on a regular basis, you will become constantly and naturally grateful. The best part of being grateful is that it seems to attract more experiences, friends, money and abundance to be grateful for. For some people I know, the process can feel like starting a cold car on an icy morning.

Here's my top 10 list for effortless access to gratitude:

1. Think about or write down at least three things that went right this morning. (Examples can include a warm shower, you had food, the car started, clean clothing was available, the dog was happy to see you, you have a job, etc.)

2. Think of your favorite color and take the next 60 seconds to notice where that color shows up around you. Enjoy the time noticing what you would ordinarily take for granted.

3. Hum, sing or just think about your favorite song. What emotion does this song bring to you? What memories or time period does this song bring to mind? Is it the music, the words or both that are so enjoyable to you? Find ways to bring this song into your life more often.

4. Make a list of your top 10 personal best moments, otherwise known as the happiest times of your life. Make a point to revisit these memories in your mind on a regular basis. Keep that list handy.

5. Make a point to say "thank you" today for small things. This can include the service you receive, a kind gesture from a stranger, or a new client who does business with you. Be sincere and look them in the eye with a smile. How does that feel?

6. Speak about good things with others. Talk about what you appreciate. Help others become aware of the power of gratitude. Find ways to build their emotions through gratitude exchanges. Ask someone else about their favorite song or their favorite memory.

7. Think about your favorite place in the whole world. Go there in your mind and experience the beauty once again. If it's hard to pick a place, bask in gratitude knowing that you are very lucky to have access to so many places and so much wonderful material.

8. At the end of the day, write down at least one thing that you are truly grateful for. Keep a little notebook by your bed and do this as a practice every night before you go to sleep.

9. Review your gratitude journal on a regular basis. Enjoy the happy memories.

10. Do the gratitude dance! Not sure what it is? Check out this wonderful little YouTube video for an uplifting experience at http://tinyurl.com/64skpp

Consider developing a daily ritual or new habit that brings awareness of appreciation into your life.

Below are a few more ideas you might consider integrating to boost gratitude:

• Set aside a specific time of day for appreciation: awakening, meals, breaks, bedtime. Create a meaningful routine and stick with it. Remember, habits take three weeks.

• Practice the HeartMath Quick Coherence Process referred to in Chapter 2: heart breathing, heart focus and thoughts of appreciation.

• Create a gratitude journal and write in it by candlelight. Post a gratitude summary. Update monthly on the same day you balance your checkbook.

• Notice others expressing sincere gratitude. Pay attention and smile as they do it.

• Identify new ways to express your thanks and experiment with them.

• Add appreciation time to meetings, meals and family gatherings.

• Catch yourself appreciating something in the present moment.

- Accept gratitude from others with sincerity.

- Rotate focus of your gratitude awareness. Make a point of checking in with your physical gratitude, your emotional health, your general health, your spiritual health. There's something to be grateful about in all of those areas.

- Deliberately pause and shift your focus to appreciation during stressed or troubled times.

- Notice gratitude on TV, in films and on the radio. Count the times people say, "Thanks" and "Thank you."

Notice all the goodness that surrounds you, and soon you'll be attracting even more. Have fun with the process and be patient with yourself as you develop this important new habit.

We are created to enjoy life. Being joyful allows us to attract more good experiences and to be of greater service to each other. Go out and spend the day seeing the beauty that surrounds you. When you do this, being grateful comes effortlessly.

Happiness on Tap

Wouldn't it be nice if we could just knock ourselves upside the head and suddenly experience a more pleasant emotional state? Interestingly enough, you can. Emotional Freedom Techniques, also known as EFT, is an amazing energy healing method that involves tapping on the body to balance the body's energy system. EFT is an innovative and effective healing modality found within the broader field referred to as Energy Psychology.

Gary Craig, the founder of EFT, believes that the cause of all negative emotions is a block or short circuit in the body's energy system. EFT tapping allows these blocks to be cleared and energy to flow and balance without re-experiencing additional pain or trauma. Think of EFT as a way to reset a breaker switch in the body's electrical system. EFT can also be used to reduce or eliminate physical symptoms or pain. Imagine how beneficial that would be for taking on a new habit, forgiving someone after a hurtful encounter or building a positive attitude for confidence in the midst of challenge. You can also use EFT to feel young, look younger than your age and maintain youthful function.

You can begin learning EFT on your own. On page 65 you will find the basic EFT self-care treatment sequence I use and share with my clients. You may also find slightly different forms of instructions via the Web, as there are many variations used by practitioners. As you learn about the points, the basic process for setting up healing statements and get started, I know you will want more resources. In Appendix III, you can find a variety of sample EFT treatment scripts for some of life's most common challenges. These include dealing with difficult people, getting over procrastination, letting go of something that's painful and relief for a food craving.

Everybody knows what their own pain is. These generic treatments are a way to get started, whether you need to let go of a craving for sugar or something unhealthy or whether you want to build a feeling of confidence or gratitude. EFT, Emotional Freedom Techniques, can help you.

Several short videos are available on at www.energymakeover4U.com to help you see what EFT looks like and tap along with me. I always recommend finding a certified practitioner to work with directly so that you gain confidence quickly. Most of my clients become quite adept at EFT self-care after three or four private or group sessions. Certified practitioners in your area may be found at **www.energypsych.org and www.EFTUniverse.com**

The Surrender Prayer

One of my favorite EFT treatment videos is called *The Surrender Prayer.* Sometimes we don't have answers to our problems. What I love about The Surrender Prayer is that it's powerful to say that you don't have the answer and that you're simply asking for relief. You can watch a short video of *The Surrender Prayer* at www.energymakeover4U.com.

It's common not to have answers. Even if you don't have the answer or have no idea what to do, you can treat yourself or facilitate treatment for a client. There's always something you can do. What is required is that you feel your pain, discomfort, and negative emotions—then ask to be helped, enlightened or empowered in some way. This is how you can face life, feel it and to make a decision that you'd like something else to replace it. It's really that simple.

Positive Emotions Activate Attraction and Success

What gets in the way of attraction? If we really want more—more money, more clients, and more joy in our lives, why doesn't it all line up immediately? Negative emotions and limiting beliefs can put up energetic road blocks. You don't have room within your energy system to attract positive things if your system is crowded with negatives! If you want to attract more, the negative must be recognized, accepted and cleared away. Only then can we choose to move to attract the positive experiences and desires.

It is the search for meaning, comfort and connection that drives successful people into action. Feeling the positive emotions that flow from the outcomes we desire brings fuel to the situation and activates the invisible to become visible. I truly believe EFT tapping is an effective way to make a positive emotional shift occur quickly. Be patient and keep tapping as you master the art of positive thought.

The Basic EFT Procedure

1. Choose a specific issue or "problem" for work. Rate the intensity, or subjective units of distress (SUDs) on a scale of 0–10

2. Create Setup Statement and reminder phrase

   "Even though I have this _____, I completely love and accept myself." Say the affirmation out loud three times while rubbing the sore spot or tapping on the Karate Chop point.

3. The Sequence: Tap about 7–10 times on each of the following points while repeating a *reminder phrase* at each point

   1) Crown or top of head
   2) Third Eye/Middle of forehead
   3) Inside edge of eyebrow
   4) Outside corners of eye
   5) Under eye on ridge of bone
   6) Center below nose/above upper lip
   7) Center below lower lip
   8) Collarbone
   9) Under arm
   10) Optional: under breast (underwire line)
   11) Hit wrists together
   12) Optional: Finger points (side of nail bed closest to you)

4. The Nine-Gamut Procedure (optional, if needed)

   Tap on the Gamut Point (furrow on hand between pinkie and ring finger) while doing these nine actions:

   1) Open eyes
   2) Close eyes
   3) Eyes hard down right
   4) Eyes down hard left
   5) Roll eyes in a circle
   6) Roll eyes in the other direction
   7) Hum two seconds of a song
   8) Count to five
   9) Hum two seconds of a song.

5. Stop and evaluation intensity on a 0-10 scale (if >0 repeat the sequence)

6. **Repeat** the sequence, if needed. Repeat the reminder phrase or adjust wording to reflect that you are addressing the remaining problem.

Strong Voice and Powerful Words

"Be not lax in celebrating.
Be not lazy in the festive service of God.
Be ablaze with enthusiasm."
Hildagard von Bingen

When you embrace the connection of mind, body and spirit as the foundation for creating optimal health, enthusiastic affirmations are a positive way to take action. Why would positive words and thoughts make such a difference to health? Affirmations mobilize emotions of optimism, which in turn keep unhealthy stress responses in check. Clinical studies have correlated optimism to the strength of our heart, long-term cancer survival, a slowed pace of aging, a stronger immune response and faster post-surgical recovery.

Be reminded that the law of attraction works because "like attracts like". Affirmations are an incredible way of putting healthy energy into motion by creating an attractor field. It becomes a magnet for attracting more—more health, more anything. It's also simple. Just practice a minute or two of positive affirmation time each day and you initiate the process to attract radiant health to your physical body. You can coach and empower yourself with affirmations through all sorts of life challenges, including health issues. Just follow these four simple steps.

1. **Accept and appreciate the now.** Find something about your health and appreciate it right now. Be grateful for the present situation. Even if you are dealing with a significant challenge, surgery, physical pain or treatment. Search deeply and you'll find something good. Speak words of appreciation. Express your acceptance for the present state. Affirmations appropriate for someone recovering from surgery or cancer treatment could include.

   - "I appreciate feeling rested when I awaken."

   - "I can comfortably push my body to do a little bit more to-day than I did yesterday."

   - "I have enough energy to walk today."

- "My digestive system is comfortable and efficient."

- "I'm alert and appreciate the people who are caring for me."

- "I enjoy having enough energy to walk."

2. **Create affirmations that express your wildest wishes.** Here's where you can have some fun. Develop a list of affirmations that express how you really wish things were. As you create these statements allow your positive emotions to amplify. What would it feel like to actually feel 20 years younger? The key is to get in touch with the joy and enthusiasm you hold for the possibility of something better. Make yourself a visually beautiful list and post it for easy reference. Leave space to add new thoughts as these come up.

Here are a few of my favorite affirmations for people longing to feel younger, healthier and more energetic:

- "I am blessed to live in a body that feels as if it were 20 years younger."

- "My body responds in wonderful ways when I make healthy choices." "I am an example of health that inspires everyone I meet."

- "I respond remarkably well to natural treatments."

- "I'm in tune with my body at all times and it feels great."

- "My skin radiates a healthy glow."

- "I'm passionate about my own health as well as the health of others."

- "I believe health miracles happen all the time, even for me."

- "I believe a healthier body starts with my positive thoughts."

- "My health radiates even as I get older."

3. **Set aside time each day to say your affirmations out loud with emotion and enthusiasm.** Amplify the power of your words by tapping on your meridian points as you speak. Refer to the point diagram on page 27 for reference. When I say you must say these affirmations out loud, that's exactly what I mean.

Say them with excitement. Use emphatic speech. Give your affirmations positive energy through positive emotion. Sprinkle in some laughter. Even if this seems silly, it's healthy, too. Emphasis on positive emotions will launch these affirmations as targets for attraction.

I love to tap on meridian points as I say each affirmation for a powerful jolt of uplifting energy. Try it and you'll be hooked.

4. **Return to step one and notice good things.** Create new statements to recognize your progress and celebrate your successes openly with others. You can be your own healing coach. You're a creator with amazing power to attract positive change. Have fun setting your health into motion as you enjoy building an optimistic vocabulary to support and sustain your health. Don't forget to share these secrets with everyone you meet. Everyone deserves radiant health.

Start an Epidemic: Contagious Emotions

How do you feel when somebody you care about steps into the room, locks eyes with you and gives you an affectionate grin? You feel pretty good, don't you? Now that you've been handed a few self-care resources to lift your emotions, why stop there? You could be the spark that lights up the room for somebody else.

The Answer to Someone's Prayer

Millions of people could use an emotional shift out of a negative rut. You could be the answer to their prayer. Years ago I remember sitting in an audience as an amazing speaker's words and energy shifted my emotional state to a new high. I thought to myself, "This speaker is extraordinary." I swear she was glowing. Everything about her, her voice, her eyes, the way she moved, and the words themselves carried this magical frequency. Her light filled and lifted every person in the room and I could not help but believe that this ability was not possible for mere mortals like me. I bowed my head and I said a silent prayer asking that someday I might be able to glow with that same kind of powerful light in the midst of a room full of people. And then I forgot about it.

In the years that followed, I began speaking as part of my work as a coach and practitioner. I will never forget that day when I completed a keynote. As I watched the audience rise from their seats with applause, I knew, without a doubt, that I had lifted their hearts. As I mingled with the crowd, one of my lifelong friends sitting in the audience stepped up to me, squeezed my hand and said, "You were glowing up there." It was then that I really understood that my silent prayer had been answered.

Emotions are contagious. Why not set the intention that you would like to start a positive epidemic, and kick it off with a big smile and your own light? When you are in a positive state and sincerely interested in helping others, you can spread that contagious energy not just to one person but throughout a ballroom filled with hundreds of people.

A study conducted by Harvard with the University of California San Diego looked at 5,000 people over a 20-year time period. The study found that emotional states are contagious, not just affecting immediate social circles but extending to friends and friends of friends. Imagine the power in that. If you speak to a room full of people, heaven knows what you're going to start with a positive message and positive emotions.

Start with just one person or a small group of friends. Pay it forward when someone gives you an energy boost. Remember, when you share your light your energy grows and amplifies. Nothing is lost. Shine brilliantly wherever you go and whenever you encounter another living creature. Count your blessings that you, too, have the power to positively change the world and the emotions of those around you.

Practice Time

1. Create three unique, positive affirmations. Write them on a 3x5 index card and tape them to your bathroom mirror or the dashboard of your car. Make sure to say them loudly and with enthusiasm each day. Speak them daily for a month, longer if you like. Pay attention to what happens.

2. Make a list of people and situations you would like to forgive and let go. Put these situations and people on a list even if you're not sure you can really do it. Pick one from your list and use the EFT treatment script for forgiveness (see Appendix III). Notice thoughts and ideas that come up as you tap. Repeat the tapping sequences and the statements until you experience a pleasant shift to a more positive state. Seek to get your relative distress down below a two, preferably down to a zero. Repeat and if you need to shift the statements to better meet your needs, do that.

3. Write a thank you note to someone you appreciate. Do it now and mail it immediately.

4. Notice a negative belief or thought that you've been holding onto, and that you have difficulty letting go. Create a positive affirmation that is the opposite of this thought. Say it out loud as you hold your hand over your heart and use heart massage to amplify the positive nature of this opposite, positive thought. How does it feel? Make a note of the shifts that you enjoy and notice.

Chapter 4

Conquer Those Energy Vampires

"Oh, my friend, it's not what they take away from you that counts.
It's what you do with what you have left."
~Hubert Humphrey

What Steals Your Energy?

Just about everyone has had an experience with an energy vampire. It may be that person who oversteps boundaries or assaults you with sabotage, a food that disagrees with you or a place that gives you the creeps. Energy vampires have a few things in common. They drain your energy, they interfere with your well-being and they mess with your state of balance.

A vampire attack can happen at work or may occur with people who share your life or your home. It can be deliberately inflicted or it can happen quite by accident. Sometimes your own habits are part of the problem, too. You don't have to put up with this kind of energy drain. Knowledge is power. Once you know how your energy flows and how to control your own energy, you are armed to conquer Those vampires.

Take a moment right now and think about those situations and people who tend to leave you feeling drained. You might want to jot some names, scenes and places down right now. Begin to understand how wise you already are, and what you already know. You don't have to understand it completely. Just try to be more aware. If nothing particular comes to mind right now, begin paying attention to your energy level throughout the day in different situations and with different people. Pay attention to how your energy goes up and also how

71

it plummets. Those unexpected times when your energy plummets can give you a lot of information about protecting yourself now and in the future. Pay attention.

Energy Toxins: Another Kind of Vampire

If you think of energy health as a process of balance and flow, energy toxins are those things that block and clog your stream of the energy flow. Energy toxins can include foods, medications, alcohol, electronic devices, and toxic substances in the environment. Things like weather and barometric pressure can also provoke energy drain. Ask anyone who suffers from a serious allergy how they feel after being exposed to the substance that causes their reaction. They'll tell you it's a miserable thing. They can go from being happy and social one minute to nauseated, choking, stuffy or uncomfortable the next. They'll tell you that a reaction provokes fear, keeps them from concentrating and often interferes with sleep and other pleasant necessities of life. That is exactly what energy toxins do!

Caroline's Story

A new client, whom I'll call Caroline, came to me several years ago complaining of intense exhaustion. It seemed like no matter where she went or what she did, she felt more and more powerless. As her story unfolded, what became clear was that there were two specific people in her life who were draining her. They were draining her big time.

One of these people happened to be her boss. During meetings, Caroline's boss would publicly sabotage her suggestions and criticize her contributions. This boss often barged into her office unannounced. She'd even sneak up on her in the hallways, make unreasonable demands and make loud, hurtful comments in public places. Sometimes just a simple glare from this woman across the hallway would send chills through Caroline's whole body. Enduring this situation on a full-time basis, day after day, was becoming nearly impossible. Caroline carried the stress home with her each night after work, too. On top of it all, Caroline was taking classes to complete her graduate degree in the evenings.

Adding to Caroline's stress was the fact that her mother-in-law had recently passed away and her husband had been named the executor of the estate. Caroline and her husband were suddenly faced with the additional responsibilities of cleaning, packing and distributing possessions according to the will, selling off remaining possessions and putting the home up for scale.

Managing every aspect of settling the estate was bad enough, but now Caroline found herself suddenly under attack from her sister-in-law, who laid claim to all sorts of items in the home. If she wanted something she would just take it, putting up a fight if Caroline resisted her demands. Caroline's husband ignored the situation while Caroline found herself crumbling to these demands. She didn't have enough energy to put any resistance into the situation after a hard day at work. Now she had very little, if any, time at all for herself.

It's no wonder Caroline was feeling so scrambled and exhausted. She was being drained from every angle. She knew what she was doing now wasn't working. She wasn't dealing with her own physical health or emotional situations very well, either. Caroline clearly knew that she had reached a time for change.

She explained her frustrations to me by saying, "I just can't walk out, I can't quit my job, I can't stop going to class, and I can't divorce my family. How can you help me be stronger? Help me deal with these people and these situations so that I can have some peace."

Caroline's story isn't unusual. Many people go into therapy and coaching arrangements with hope of dealing with their surroundings and the people in their lives in a better way. Energy awareness and taking care of your own energy situation can make an enormous difference in how you experience others in your world. Sometimes it's not clear where your energy boundary begins and ends. We have physical bodies but our energy goes out beyond that. Because we are part of a holographic world, our energy ebbs and flows and connects with the energies of everything out there in the world.

Free flowing energy can be a good thing. Energy can bring us intuition, help us to be of higher service, allow us to engage in our world and even help us notice things when we're supposed to notice them so that we can be fully present and fully ourselves.

In the case of energy vampires like Caroline's boss and her sister-in-law, we know that being under that kind of attack is unpleasant, yet it's a common human experience. Those energy vampires can suddenly come in and lower our energy state without warning. Those sudden attacks are the ones that are most memorable and I'm sure you can think of a moment from your past when your energy level dropped as if a cable in an elevator had suddenly been cut.

Preparing for Hostile Territory

By recognizing what causes an energy drain you can become more aware and more resilient so that you can get through those situations without such a drop in your energetic state. First of all, knowing that energy vampires are teachers and the lessons they teach us can be painful but they usually show us something about ourselves that is very much connected to our life purpose and our mission here. We need to pay attention. Sometimes the only thing that gets our attention is pain.

So what do these energy vampires want and what do they do? Energy vampires can blindside you. They unexpectedly come up with something out of left field that totally throws you for a loop. They jump you when you are vulnerable and unprepared. Energy vampires can use mean words and often choose the words that hurt the most and the deepest. Energy vampires love public drama. The more drama the better. It's almost as if the drama puts fuel on their fire, even as it takes the energy away from you.

Vampires often enjoy the attention their outbursts draw. Their energy gets a boost when you have an outburst in response to their provocation. Some outbursts can be so loud that it's embarrassing or makes you tremble.

Energy vampires may cry and use tears to pull you in. Energy vampires can also lie, cheat and do despicable things that they know are wrong just to get a reaction from you.

Energy vampires love power struggles. They are trying to establish themselves as the party with the highest power controlling an interaction. You don't have to let that happen. Obviously that's what they want and they will fight until they get it. In some cases, energy vampires become physically violent. This is an intolerable situation and in today's world it requires some outside help. If that is part of your experience you need to bring in a friend, a protector or call 9-1-1 for your personal safety. In the United States, you can get help by calling the National Domestic Violence Hotline at 1-800-799-SAFE (7233) or www.thehotline.org. You should never, ever have to tolerate a violent situation. Please keep that in mind. There are many resources to help people involved in domestic violence and other forms of hostile abuse, even in the workplace. Don't remain silent.

Beware of the Stealth Vampires

There can be energy vampires who are subtle and hard to detect. Perhaps you are someone who finds yourself feeling drained when in crowds. That's a situation where you've got the collective force of others pulling from you and invading your energy space. You don't have to be engaged in a conflict to feel violated. Low energy individuals can tap into your energy field at any time and drain off some of your energy. Energy fields can mingle and intersect, too. You may find yourself picking up subtle psychic messages, physical sensations or awareness of emotions during crowd experiences. These are energetic exchanges that exist all the time as part of normal social interactions.

Certain settings can trigger energy loss, too— not because somebody intended it to happen, but because your energy system may be vulnerable to the social mixture of the place you put yourself in. Crowds scramble boundaries and they can make energy shifts more intense. People who work in large public places such as schools, health care facilities and large organizations need to be particularly aware of that powerful stealth energy coming in and out of their workplace every day.

Just being aware of it is the first step in helping yourself become resilient to a crowd situation. Honor your sensitivity. It is okay to experience the energy shifts when they happen. Low energy people will pull energy from others because they are low and they need more energy. They sense a higher energetic state nearby and they're drawn to it. They clip themselves into your energy field and pull it into theirs, often without regard to you or where it's coming from.

Sometimes it can be malicious and sometimes it's completely unintentional. Those people are just so low that they're pulling energy simply to survive. In either case, love them and know that the state they're in is not very pleasant for them either. You're both going through something painful together.

Handle the Energy Vampires with Grace

By reading this chapter you're already much more aware than you used to be. Take some time to write down your own energy invasion experiences. Know your history.

- What happens to you on a daily basis?

- When are you most likely to have an energy loss happen?

- Is there a time of day when you're most vulnerable to attack?

- What other situations bring on more energy drain for you?

- Is it when you are at work?

- Is it when you're at home or during family gatherings?

- Is it during gatherings with certain people?

- Is it during certain times of the year or particular holidays?

- Notice the patterns of who, what, when, where, why and how.

In the case of Caroline, she was clearly aware of two distinct vampires. She knew the WHO invading her system but she had no idea how to deal with them. If you're able to identify the *who* or the *what*, that's a big help. Then you can begin to develop a strategy to deal with that person. Notice the patterns and especially notice your own pattern of vulnerability. That's how you can make changes occur.

Notice Your Current Response Pattern

Obviously you play a role in any given situation. Perhaps you are unwillingly or unknowingly giving up your energy by just handing it over. One response pattern is to be totally silent and to take a beating, literally or figuratively. You become a victim and they become an attacker who takes and takes and takes. Once you've developed a reputation for that kind of response, the minute you change things you're going to shake things up. Your attacker will be mystified.

I had a client who was having trouble at work. She was being taken advantage of and allowed it to continue for a good decade or so. She asked for help with energy boundaries. When I offered her a few practical suggestions for approaching this situation differently, her response was, "They won't know what to think of that. They only know me as somebody who takes a beating, who resigns herself to what's thrown at her and who just does what they say. They'll be so shocked. They'll think there's something wrong with me. I can already anticipate those strange looks they're going to give me when I say no."

I said to her, "So what? It's time to protect yourself. You asked for a change. What do you expect?" You, too, must initiate a change in order to get a better experience.

Think about what you're doing right now. Are you engaging in battle? Are you adding to the drama? Are you putting yourself in situations where you might be able to completely opt out? That's the power of saying "NO." If you're not saying "no" to situations that are optional, that is something you can change. It requires a backbone and some intention to do it. You do have the power.

What about Vampires in the Family?

In the case of family members or others who are going to be part of your life for a long time, you need to look at your responses to them, too. Is there a way you can reduce your exposure to them? Professional counseling or mediation can also be helpful to begin meaningful resolution. You are responsible and can control your side of these relationships through words, action, listening and asking for or offering help. Your feelings are your truth. The same can be said for the other person. As I mentioned before, when violence is involved please reach out for help. Don't go through this alone.

Connect to Divine Protection through Prayer

There is divine help out there for you, too. Often prayer is the very best answer to an energy drain problem. Simply surrender it to a higher power. Ask God (Divine source, or whatever term you feel most comfortable using) to help you. Ask God to give you the words that bring you divine intervention, words that might help the other person to settle down in your midst. Ask God to give that vampire energy from another source instead of taking it from you.

If you believe in a higher power, that higher power has the ability to provide unlimited energy so you can keep yours. Allow yourself to become a conduit of energy from the Divine so that you are able to give that low energy vampire as much energy as they need. Ask that your system be replenished on a constant basis from that Divine source. Asking really works. Even if you don't believe it will help, ask anyway.

Expect the Best

Energy flows where intentions go. Sometimes we expect bad things from people who have not even behaved badly yet. Have you ever gone into a meeting or situation thinking somebody was going to raise a royal fit and braced yourself for it only to have them come in with a good mood? Probably not. If you expect people to raise a royal fit or give you trouble and be full of objections that might be exactly what you receive.

Be careful about what you are expecting, what you are intending and where you are putting your thoughts. You have the opportunity to change a situation by simply expecting the best. Forgive others ahead of time and expect a miracle. It just might happen. Perhaps your vampire will come into the room a little less agitated and a little higher in their energy so they don't have to take yours.

Effective managers soon discover that if you expect the best of your people, they will rise to meet your expectations and often they will exceed them. Use positive expectation as a way of building up every person you encounter and they are apt to show you their very best side.

Install Your Diamond Shield™

The Diamond Shield is a powerful metaphor for the process of fortifying your energy. It is one that I refer to often when I speak and coach. It is one of those fashion accessories I will not go out without. It has nothing to do with jewelry and it costs nothing to wear. Why is a shield so important? Everything is energy. However, we need not expose ourselves to everything. We need a good barrier or a filter to keep our own energy clean. Forces, situations and people in our environment can drain energy.

Unfortunately our energy will at times be intentionally invaded by others. This shield is a defensive mechanism to deliberately contain our energy, create healthy boundaries and prevent leaks. Our discerning intention installs and activates this protective energy barrier.

Here's my simple recipe for creating your customized Diamond Shield:

1. **Container of light.** As you begin the day, intentionally see yourself inside a container or bubble of sparkling bright light.

2. **Zip up.** Do this by placing the palm of your right hand facing your body, about one to two inches from your pelvic bone. Imagine that you are zipping up a big zipper from your pelvic bone, up your midline and stopping as you touch the point on your chin just under the lower lip. Bring the hand away from the body after you touch the lip and return that right hand to the place above the pelvic bone and zip up two more times for a total of three zips. By tracing the central meridian you are reinforcing your energy boundary and the healthy flow of central meridian energy. This central meridian crosses your heart vertically and often the heart is the energy center where those vampires are going to steel energy from you. By zipping up you're protecting that vulnerable place within your energy system.

3. **Set your boundaries.** Take a deep breath and consider the boundaries you may need to hold in place during the day ahead. What must you say no to? What must you do to conserve your energy? What is your bottom line when it comes to how you allow others to treat you and how you treat yourself? These are the rules of engagement. Make sure your intentions are kind and accept them as your way of nurturing and loving yourself while communicating to others how you desire to be treated.

4. **Sit tall and place thumbs inside your closed fist.** Sitting tall boosts your mood and your confidence. Qi Gong Master Robert Peng recommends keeping the thumb inside the closed fist as a way to strengthen the energetic boundary and the intentions you have set in step 3 above.

5. **Magnify your light.** Set an intention that the Diamond Shield™ you have installed will magnify your light and allow others to

see the highest and best in you. Think about how diamonds so beautifully reflect light. And so it is with you.

6. **Illuminate others.** Believe that while the Diamond Shield™ protects you it also allows you to see the light in others even when that light is low or faint. Even the most depressed or nasty person can radiate when seen through a diamond. The diamond provides both magnification of the light and the potential for the highest and best to be seen instead of missed. The diamond also allows a low energy individual to see the reflection of their own light coming off the diamond, boosting their own sense of self.

Allow the Diamond Shield™ to serve and teach you as you go through life. Help others use it to build energy during difficult times. Appreciate how it enhances your experiences of daily living. Wear your shield in good health and radiate love.

Notice and Re-Adjust Your Energy

When you're dealing with energy vampires, recognize that they can be a nasty bunch and you may have to try a few different ways of fortifying your energy field before you have the results you'd hoped for. The key in all of this is to pay attention. Pay attention to yourself. Practice good self-care before you even encounter these people. Make sure you're installing your Diamond Shield™ and that you are setting good intentions. Be clear about your part of the encounter before you're in the midst of it. A little pre-planning can go a long way. Draw upon your intuitive hunches to change or adjust your responses as you go. Be curious. Test a variety of responses and notice what happens. Keep track of what works and what doesn't. Focus on active, continuous improvement.

Fortify Your Fortress

Sometimes we go into these encounters with energy vampires with low energy reserves. If we are already drained that's asking for trouble. If you are most vulnerable at the end of the day, what does that tell you? If you have done things during the day to deplete your energy, one mean look or a nasty comment from somebody may suddenly take your energy down to the basement.

You do your best energy management with a Diamond Shield™ when you are well rested, have taken time for yourself, have been engaged doing something you love or when you have taken a moment to reflect with gratitude or appreciation. You can become especially resilient to energy attack when you have cleared negative memories, emotions or beliefs by tapping on your EFT energy meridian points.

You're also better protected when you have consistently eaten a healthy, balanced diet and when we're fully hydrated with water. These physical factors contribute to our protective walls of the energy fortress and they can make a difference between a very positive encounter with a low energy person or a disastrous one.

I remind you, fortify your fortress to be fully ready before you go into a treacherous, energy draining situation. Yes, put on your Diamond Shield and do everything in your power to be strong physically, mentally, spiritually and energetically so that you can handle whatever comes up. That's true resilience.

Reopen Your Broken Heart and Shine

One of the reasons that we aren't more fully effective as energetic beings in the world is that we have become broken and closed hearted. It is human to be emotionally attacked and wounded over the course of a lifetime. We suffer each time that dagger of anger, grief, blame or rejection tears into our heart and pulls it apart. With each vulnerable heart wound the next encounter with another insensitive, low energy person agitates that wound even further.

In self-defense, closing the heart stops the pain but it denies access to those wonderful people who offer true love. That is perhaps the greatest heart pain and wound of all.

Consider the possibility that having a closed heart throughout a lifetime will never allow you to fully tap into the infinite source of energy. Don't you want an infinite line that's always there to give you all the energy you need? We as humans don't connect to it as often as we could, but it's there and it's ready for you when you open your heart.

In order to be fully connected, the heart has to be open, yet that seems so vulnerable. As you work with the Diamond Shield™, you

81

will confidently and reliably have this line of energy running through you more of the time.

Like a huge line of credit that you just grab whenever you need it, whether somebody unexpectedly starts drawing from your supply, it's there automatically. You do your part by shielding yourself daily before you go into the world and by taking good care of yourself. By simply being aware and by being the loving, open-hearted person that you are, you will remain strong.

How to Open Your Heart

Begin by opening your heart to things that are easy to love. Consider loveable examples like pets, babies, a grandchild, your own children, or a reliable friend who has never let you down. Breathe deeply. Feel your heart beating and appreciate that you own the capacity to love infinitely. There are people who can be that force for you so that you can have the experience of being open-hearted and safe. If you don't think they exist, ask for them to enter your life. Set the intention through prayer. Remember, you are the answer to someone else's prayer.

A Happy Ending for Caroline

Several months after Caroline and I began working together, I noticed an amazing change in her. Caroline began using her energy boundary effectively through intentional awareness. She began eating more fresh fruits and vegetables, drinking more water and practicing a daily energy routine. She did the Diamond Shield™ exercises, which included "zipping-up" three times through her central meridian before work each day. She looked in the mirror daily before going out, used positive affirmations and became more aware of her capacity for love and compassion. She prayed for assistance in maintaining a state of inner peace, no matter what was going on in the world around her.

As Caroline's energy self-care became a habit, she was able to ask for what she needed. She eventually approached her superiors at work and filed the appropriate paperwork to document the way her boss had been mistreating her. Subsequently, her boss was held accountable and was eventually demoted for her unprofessional behavior. It required work on Caroline's part, but in the end Caroline was assigned to a new boss, given additional responsibility and is now thriving at work, doing what she loves in a job that is better suited to her.

On Caroline's personal side, time healed a lot of things. Death in the family is a difficult emotional experience compounded by the need to deal with dividing an estate. As time passed, Caroline reported that the family found peace in distributing the possessions of her husband's mother. It was not always easy, but Caroline decided to let go of worrying about small things. Caroline willingly surrendered a few items to her sister-in-law to maintain the peace, yet she also stood up for herself when something really mattered. She asked for what she needed. She expressed her feelings to her sister-in-law in a kind and factual way.

Remember, when you express your feelings, you are always right. They are your feelings. Nobody else can tell you what your feelings are. Caroline finally learned that important lesson. Caroline got through this challenging time because she was willing to change. She is convinced that energy awareness made all the difference in the world. She's now regularly using EFT tapping for self-care and uses the Diamond Shield™ as part of every day, even though she has very few conflicts with other people. Her marriage is thriving and other relationships are positive. Those kinds of great things happen when you get your energy boundaries in order.

Energy vampires are out there, but you don't have to suffer. Take a lesson from Caroline. Adjust, be yourself, speak up, set boundaries and then let go. As your heart opens to just a single possibility, your heart opens to everything. That's the miracle that's possible through energy. You will always have a high supply of energy with an open, shielded heart.

Be Conscious of How You Affect the Energy of Others

Everyone needs to be reminded now and then that they, too, can become an energy vampire. This is especially important if you are in an influential or leadership position. I was made mindful of this through a segment of the radio program This American Life that aired on National Public Radio. The program was about people in powerful roles like teachers, bosses, therapists, judges and parents who didn't give much thought, awareness or responsibility regarding the people they had power over.

Be careful not to judge, criticize or make your clients, students, suppliers or employees feel small in any way. Be a resource and someone who suggests ideas, enforces policy, but rarely dictates action. Leadership is a sacred trust that allows you to work with others. Be careful not to betray it. Lead from a place of humble consciousness.

As a boss and a business manager it is your job to put intention into being fair, diplomatic and an example for others. If you enforce rules, you certainly must follow them. Leading by example is the best way to communicate what you expect.

Being a parent requires consciousness too. Now that my children are grown, I observe them doing things without me watching and I'm proud that they have chosen to live by the values my husband and I demonstrated for them.

Think about who you have power over and take it seriously. As you find yourself in a place where you can choose who your leaders will be, also be mindful of who you give your power to. Remember that responsibility matters and integrity is essential. The best leaders inspire by example. I'm always watching for that kind of leader. I know you will, too.

Practice Time

1. Who is invading your energy? List some names. When does it happen? Are there times when you are particularly vulnerable? Jot down a story of one of your energy vampire invasions. What you can learn from something that's already happened?

2. How will you prepare for your next encounter with one of the specific energy vampires you mentioned? Write down the action you plan to take before your next meeting. Make sure to also add notes about how your encounter went after it's all over. What did you learn? What did you experience as a result of your preparation? Was anything different?

3. What kind of leaders or role models do you choose to give your power to? Jot down a few qualities that you value in a responsible leader.

4. What will you do in the next 30 days to ensure that you have a constant supply of vibrant energy? What will you do to make sure that the energy vampires are taken care of, yet your energy remains strong and never depleted?

Chapter 5

Slender, Young,
Glowing and Intuitive

*"The pursuit of truth and beauty is a sphere of activity in which we are
permitted to remain children all our lives."*
Albert Einstein

What Does Everyone Want?

Everybody really wants the same thing. We want to be cared for,
acknowledged, accepted and included. We want to be part of the
bigger picture in some way, right? On the most primitive level it
means being safe, having our physical needs met, and having enough
money to survive. As those basic needs are met we naturally want
more. We also want to be loved, respected, attractive, healthy, afflu-
ent, accepted or considered significant in some way. We want to be
comfortable and also noticed enough so that we can make a difference in this lifetime.

What if there was a pill to unlock the 80 percent of your brain
power that some experts claim humans fail to use? The ability to do
amazing things like solve complex problems, read minds and intuitively know the best answer at any given moment—that would be
pretty wonderful indeed. Most of us would certainly want that too.

How can we do a better job at claiming and attracting the safety,
comfort, love, money, intuition and significance we want so much?
The law of attraction says there's enough for everyone, yet getting
our fair share seems so hard.

Women Have to Work Harder!

We women burn up lots of energy working on those physical elements that help us both fit in and stand out. You know what I mean—hair, makeup, clothing, manicures, diets, accessories and shoes. We've been conditioned to believe that we must be slender, young, beautiful, smart and nice in order to be worthy of attention, comfort and economic stability. Somehow love was left out of this picture. You know exactly what I'm saying, don't you? We have been cultured into a physical world that doesn't allow for imperfections or flaws in our physical traits in spite of the fact that we are surrounded by a different reality.

It is okay to be confused. I suffer from it, too. As a marketer, speaker and entrepreneur, I have spent considerable time and money working on my professional image. I've spent those moments in front of the mirror thinking some nasty things—just like you. I worry about how I look in photos, on the stage and in videos. I beat myself up trying to be the best version of myself that I can possibly be. As a woman over 50, it feels like I need more "spackle" than I used to in order to pull it off.

All kidding aside, it is my sincere desire to look and feel healthy, attractive, slender, more interesting, happier and younger than the other people my age. All those physical things are important values to me. It shouldn't matter, but it really does matter! Consequently, I have decided to accept my values as the truth. I know you probably want more of these qualities, too. So give yourself permission to be just as superficial as I am. Go ahead and want more. This chapter will help you reach for more.

Winning at Waist Management™ with Energy

Look around. We intuitively know that people with slim middles and flat tummies are the healthy ones. They look fit and attractive. They're the athletes, the young ones, the women who haven't had kids yet and the men who sport those six pack abs instead of lounging on the couch drinking six packs.

But wait a minute. Look again. Kids seem to be carrying more weight around their middles these days. Young women who haven't yet carried a child are sporting a pouch out front. Little boys have belly rolls, too. What's up with that? Should we be concerned? The answer is yes.

Modern medical science has provided ample evidence that carrying excess weight around the waistline correlates strongly with health risk, and can be predictive of health problems, including early death.

For women, excess waistline girth is associated with diabetes, heart disease, infertility and ovarian cancer. Women with a waist-hip ratio of 0.7 have optimal estrogen levels and are less susceptible to major disease and health problems.

Belly fat in men also correlates with increased diabetes, cardiovascular disorders, and prostate and testicular cancers. Men with waist-hip ratios of around 0.9 are likewise shown to be more healthy, fertile and resistant to disease and cancer.

Two Kinds of Belly Fat

There really are two kinds of fat that add to your waistline. The first type is subcutaneous fat, which is the fat just under your skin. Subcutaneous fat shows up as dimples and cellulite. This is the kind you even see on babies.

The second type of fat, visceral fat, surrounds your vital organs deep within your abdomen. Visceral fat is associated with health problems and inflammation. While diet is one way to reduce inflammation and visceral fat, aerobic exercise has proven to be the most rapid and effective way to reduce the waistline inches associated with this high-risk visceral fat.

WHR: The New Health Standard

The evidence now available suggests that waist hip ratio (WHR) is far more predictive of health risk than body mass index (BMI). Although BMI is the current standard used for defining obesity, if obesity was redefined with WHR instead, there would be a three-fold increase in the early detection of human health risk.

Your Waistline: A Measure of Attraction and Mate Selection

Humans have evolved to some extent, but we are still primitive when it comes to noticing each other. Models and body builders with slim middles get our attention. The waist hip ratio is sending subtle cues to the world with regard to a person's fertility and suitability as a mate. Women with that healthy 0.7 WHR are consistently considered attractive, although the weight behind the number can vary in a large degree. Body types as diverse as Marilyn Monroe, Twiggy, Jennifer Lopez and Sophia Loren have an attractive WHR in common.

The same is true for men. Women are highly attracted to those guys with the healthy 0.9 waist hip ratio. We all want to choose partners who will be fertile and healthy enough so that we might enjoy our golden years together.

Most people know what must be done to possess a smaller waistline. It usually requires change, struggle, effort, pain and work. If it were easy we would all have healthy, slim waist hip ratios. We know that making healthy food choices, cutting down on portions, exercising more and giving up fatty, sugary, delicious treats will bring us closer to a healthy waistline.

Success requires planning, asking for help, anticipating temptation and getting back on track when we mess up. We need help sticking with a plan, managing life's stress and staying motivated. Fortunately, that is where the use of daily energy self-care and Emotional Freedom Techniques (EFT) provides a key. By adding these tools to the process of change the discomfort is much more subtle, and healthy choices can be made with a clear mindfulness.

For a more comprehensive discussion of self-care guidance to trim your middle, please check out my book *Winning at Waist Management*™ available on Amazon Kindle. You can also download a free *Winning at Waist Management*™ starter kit at www.energymakeover4U.com

Below are my top 10 tips for combining energy self-care with a successful Waist Management™ program:

1. **Measure your waist hip ratio** regularly and keep track of it monthly. Set the intention that you want to move closer to that ideal healthy ratio, which is 0.7 for women and 0.9 for men. A video to help you take this measurement properly can be found at www.energymakeover4U.com

2. **Seek support.** Find a buddy who also wants a healthier waist hip ratio and agree to work together. Share your goals, your favorite healthy recipes, exercise time and discuss your emotions, too. Joining a formal support group like Weight Watchers or an exercise class is an excellent plan.

3. **Move energy to your belly.** Stress puts way too much energy in our heads, yet our physical center is closer to the gut. One of the best ways to quickly get out of your head is to close your eyes and breathe. As long as you are not driving you can do this almost anywhere and at any time. Try belly breathing—see the box below for details.

Belly Breathing 101

- Place both hands on your belly over your navel.

- Inhale expanding your belly first, then moving the air up into the lungs. Keep your shoulders down and feel your belly press against your hands.

- Exhale, bringing your belly in. Imagine that your belly button is pressed against your spine as you fully release your breath

- Repeat for two to five minutes. Integrate belly breathing at stop lights or whenever you are on hold or waiting is a practical way to lose inches from your waistline. This is also a great stress reliever

---

4. **Choose water as your #1 beverage.** You already know water is healthy, helps conduct energy and that you need it to have a clear mind. When it comes to Waist Management™ most drinks other than water carry some sort of negative quality that will set you back. Coffee with cream and sugar carries extra calories, fat and caffeine. Soft drinks and juices have added sugar. Diet drinks have an assortment of chemicals that you're better off without. Alcoholic beverages are full of calories, carry little nutritional value and can endanger your safety, too. While you might indulge occasionally in a glass of wine or a daily latte, realize that all these little extras add up over time. You'll save money and your waistline by choosing water instead.

5. **Own your emotions and tap** on your feelings, cravings and difficult challenges. We may be eating fat, salt and sugar to soothe frazzled nerves, hurt feelings, loneliness or sadness. Even when we make healthy food choices, we may feel deprived and denied. Feelings are real, and the sooner you admit them, accept them and tap on them, the more successful you will be. That goes well beyond your waistline.

6. **Pause and Take Breaks.** Catch yourself in those moments when you have a choice, and just stop. Close your eyes; breathe and check in with your feelings - then choose. I guarantee that you will make better choices. Research has also shown that people who take short breaks and stand frequently during their day are able to maintain smaller waistlines and maintain lower levels of C-reactive protein in their blood, a predictor of dangerous inflammation and heart disease.

7. **Switch to alkaline water.** Making a simple shift to alkaline water made a difference for me. When I made the shift to my new water filtration system in the fall of last year, I easily dropped four pounds without thinking much about it. Simultaneously my workouts became much more comfortable too. I recommend the Nikken PiMag unit, an affordable and portable gravity filtration system. A variety of alkaline water systems are available and you are encouraged to do your research before deciding which is best for you. Learn more about the Nikken PiMag System I use at www.nikken.com/product/technology/#piMagWater

8. **Get more sleep.** People not getting sufficient rest, especially those getting less than six hours, are prone to additional weight gain around the waistline due to two hormones: leptin and ghrelin. According to Michael Breus PhD, director of the Atlanta School of Sleep Medicine, "When you don't get enough sleep, it drives leptin levels down, which means you don't feel as satisfied after you eat. Lack of sleep also causes ghrelin levels to rise, which means your appetite is stimulated, so you want more food." When in doubt—go to bed!

9. **Keep track of the good stuff.** Being positive and keeping your thoughts optimistic increases success in all areas of your life. Hang out with positive people, be a positive person and infuse your day with positive thoughts. We'll keep covering

that throughout the rest of this book. Attitude makes a difference.

10. **Move Your Body.** Exercise will help your Waist Management™ program really take off, especially if you commit to at least 30 minutes every day. Energetically, exercise builds muscle, boosts your metabolic rate so you'll burn more calories and helps your body produce neurotransmitters that help you fight off depression. Find several forms you enjoy so you don't get bored doing the same thing. Having a buddy to exercise with you will motivate you on the days you're not feeling up to it. That buddy can be your dog, a neighbor, friend or somebody you meet in a class. I personally endorse Jazzercise (www.jazzercise.com) as a practical program that includes cardio, strength and flexibility training. You'll soon see a smaller waistline and variety of good results in many areas of in your life as you move that body.

Energy for Clear, Youthful Skin

Beginning at the age of 12, I became a victim of chronic acne, blotchy skin and embarrassment. Over the years I have visited more dermatologists, aestheticians, and specialists than I like to admit. I have tried everything from antibiotics, masks, sun lamps, retin-A, topical creams, nutritional supplements, acid peels, microdermabrasion, laser resurfacing and more. Nothing really worked for me. It seemed the more money I spent the redder and more irritated my face became.

I always attributed my skin problems to stress, however when I gave up my office job and pursued my new calmer life as a personal coach and EFT practitioner, my acne continued even as my stress melted away. I remember creating a vision board with the statement, "Blemish free skin," boldly printed across it. Unfortunately, as I reached my late 40s, my definition of blemishes now also included wrinkles and sagging skin. Yes, that perfect skin was what I wanted, but I remained unsure how to get it, especially because I was so sensitive to everything.

At last, something new came into my awareness. At a networking event I was approached by a woman holding a gadget that looked like a cell phone in her hand. My eyes were drawn to it and I asked,

"What is it?" She explained that it was the Galvanic Spa, a personal skin care device. It was something I could use at home to deliver micro current, moisture and anti-aging ingredients to the skin.

This little device promised to visibly reduce wrinkles and perk up your skin in about 10 minutes. I thought to myself that this sounded vaguely familiar. When I used to work at the group medical practice, we provided facials that used micro current. I'd had several of them. While they didn't clear up my acne, my skin always had a nice glow and tightness to it after I had one of those treatments. The main problem with those treatments was that you had to keep coming back week after week to retain the results. Fortunately I didn't have to pay for them as an employee, but if I was paying for them, it would have been about $75 a visit. The time, travel and money to maintain the good results were hardly a bargain. Suddenly I realized that getting my hands on a home device to give myself a facial a couple times a week for 10 minutes was definitely of interest.

I scheduled a demonstration facial the following weekend. I remember the embarrassment I felt taking off all my make-up to have this demonstration. I refused to allow a before picture to be taken. The device came with a 30-day money back guarantee, and so went home that day with the galvanic spa, enough supplies to work on my face for 30 days and a healthy dose of skepticism. I figured I had nothing to lose. I might as well have 30 days of free facials.

Within the first 10 days, my blemishes cleared up. Immediately my face had a nice smooth texture and healthy glow. I always felt really good after I performed the twice-weekly treatments every Tuesday and Saturday. It really did take less than 10 minutes to give myself this treatment. People started noticing and asking what I was using.

I eventually enrolled as a distributor and have been delighted to share this amazing little tool with hundreds of friends and colleagues, both as a business opportunity and as a beauty essential.

Today I keep using my Galvanic Spa and recommend it to anyone, young or old, who wants to maintain healthy skin. You can learn more about the Galvanic Spa with AgeLOC at http://www.betsy-muller.nsedreams.com.

The Amazing Power of Humor and Silliness

It is time for me to admit something very serious right now. I am highly suspicious of anyone or any situation that is totally without a sense of humor. You probably know the kind of people I'm referring to: rigid, stoic gurus and religious types who take themselves and everybody else way too seriously. When humor is lacking, I seriously wonder if God has left the building. My God is probably more like the jolly grinning statue of Buddha or a silly puppy who wants to endlessly lick you as you giggle.

Humor has the power to restore balance when life gets out of whack. Even in the darkest moments, humor can be like a warm blanket on a cold night, wrapping a situation in a healing presence. What does humor have to do with energy, health, spirituality and being the very best you? Humor and that child-like silliness help keep all of this energy, science, fact and drama in perspective. By the way, there are plenty of clinical studies that support the positive effects of optimism, humor and laughter on health. You don't have to look far too see the connection.

I remember a time when my own beliefs about humor were challenged. I was leading a group in the study of Eckhart Tolle's, *A New Earth*, a very deep, spiritual book. I had come to regard Mr. Tolle as a serious spiritual teacher, but regrettably thought humor and lightness were suspiciously lacking in his works. Fortunately, I had the opportunity to finally see Mr. Tolle interact with Oprah as part of a telecast. It was there that I experienced Mr. Tolle working in the live environment and finally saw the gentle, genuine soul with a very subtle silliness running through him. My awareness tells me that his God is the same one that speaks to me. I forgave myself for judging him so harshly.

Humor is an amazing healing gift. Adults have a tendency to take things way too seriously, let life get heavy and miss all the funny stuff that really is a treat to giggle about. How can we get it back? Simply setting intention and paying attention will usually do it. Be willing to do your part to bring it in. Rent funny videos, watch comedies or attend stand-up performances. If you need an instant boost there are usually some very funny videos on YouTube.com, and they're available 24/7.

Set the intention that you would like to laugh more, and think about what makes you laugh. Notice what shows up. This is great material for journaling. Hang out with silly people and encourage them to be even sillier. If you can't be funny, be a good audience.

Someone once said that wearing a smile is really the best anti-aging make-up. Having humor in your life will guarantee that smile and that inner glow will always radiate out to the world. How easy is that? Yes, there are times to be serious and life will give you plenty of them. Just keep yourself in touch with laughter, humor and silliness so that you have access to a quick boost of balance, as needed.

Become a Practical Intuitive

Intuition is a magic, mystical quality that offers each of us an inner compass, a sense of direction and guidance when making choices. It works for the best outcomes and provides a way to make decisions quickly, even when data and hard facts are missing. Everyone has used it from time to time, but most people don't trust theirs enough. I'm amazed at the number of people who want to hand me money to give them intuitive guidance instead of just trusting their own onboard system. I have been known to get angry at times with clients who have been too lazy to bother with developing their own intuitive muscles, in spite of the fact that I can show them how to activate their guiding system quickly and easily.

Perhaps caution is in order. If you become reliably intuitive there is responsibility to act on it. That can be a huge challenge to otherwise logical, left-brained, scientific types. I know. I used to be one of them. I'm also proof that people can change.

Energy Flow Activates Intuition

Want to activate intuition and be more intuitive? Get your energy moving. It really is that simple. I didn't realize this back in 2000 when I started doing the five Tibetan Fountain of Youth exercises on a daily basis. I thought I was just activating my endocrine system for a good stretch and a balance of my body's energy system. Coincidently, as I did the exercises, I was getting hunches, information, dreams and guidance of all sorts coming into my awareness both day and night. It was initially very new and strange, especially because I had not really asked for any of it.

It all happens for a reason. I soon realized that this new sensitivity I was developing was opening doors for where I was going next. It was good and I could live with it. In the years from 2000 to 2005 I played with energy self-care in a casual fashion, doing my five Tibetan exercises every day but not caring for my energy, emotions or body as consistently as I do now. Sometimes the intuition would work and other times it would fail me miserably.

This was a time when I was practicing energy more like a recreational drug than a way of being. There were these intense highs as well as crashing lows. The balance in between was harder to maintain. In 2005 when I finally quit my job and embarked on a new life as an energy coach, EFT practitioner and speaker, I began a steady practice of energy self-care. I found myself using EFT tapping sequences many times a day, both while working with clients and for my own self-care. I also invested in using HeartMath software and began training myself to hold a state of coherent heart rate variability.

As I became very proficient in holding that coherent state, it seemed my intuition grew further, while my ups and downs leveled into a smoother experience that never took me too far from that comfortable balance point. Adding a weekly yoga class to my routine brought additional benefits as I realized how easy it was to let go and just be present to difficult situations.

With intuition flowing, my biggest block became acting on it, which usually meant saying or doing something when a strange notion came up in my life or during a client session. It meant going off the standard treatment sequence, taking a new direction, asking a specific question or doing something that seemed to be nonsense.

What I found was that by taking those chances with intuition, I was acting in highest service for the clients and myself, even when it didn't make sense to me. That's how I knew to keep doing it even if it didn't make sense to my brain.

Five Ways to Activate More Intuition

1. Seriously commit to practicing at least two of the healthy energy habits discussed in chapter one.

2. Try the intuitive tongue testing technique for simple decisions. Terence C. Wade, PhD, and Darlene K. Wade, MSW, psychotherapists in private practice in Honolulu, Hawaii, developed the kinesthetic self-testing technique that is based on the idea that the body's neurological system and indicator muscles are stronger in the presence of a true or positive thought. In this case the

Intuitive Tongue Testing

- Relax your jaw and allow your tongue to float in the center of your mouth, not touching the roof, lower teeth or either side.

- Ask your subconscious to show you a "yes" or a "true" by moving your tongue either up or down. Simply think something like, "Dear subconscious, I would like you to move my tongue to show me the direction for "yes". You might also think of something you love and notice where your tongue moves. Likewise, ask your subconscious to show you the direction for "no". Begin with known true and false statements, e.g., your name and some other neutral fictitious name, to calibrate the technique before using it with statements or questions with unknown answers. "My name is (your name)," and observe your tongue movement. Next think, "My name is (neutral fictitious name)," and again observe your tongue movement.

- Test other statements or questions via your subconscious tongue test using simple "true/yes" or "false/no" questions.

- A few quick energy corrections may be needed if the initial calibration does not work consistently. Try the deep breathing, cross crawl or collar bone tapping mentioned in Chapter 1. Make sure you are hydrated by drinking a glass of water.

- Reliable testing requires practice and a relaxed state of mind. Be patient and consistent in your practice. Soon you will be much more solidly connected to intuitive feelings and may no longer need to focus on your tongue to determine the answer.

tongue is used as the test muscle. I have found this technique to be easy to teach, and is so empowering because it is private, self-administered and can be done just about anywhere. (See details in box)

3. Everyone is intuitive—even you. Most people don't trust their intuition. Find friends and family members curious about developing intuition and try the following exercises:

Stone Game: Have each player find an interesting stone and keep it in their pocket for at least a day to fully integrate the stone with their energy. Randomly have participants place each stone on a blank piece of paper so that only the stone's original owner knows which stone is theirs. As participants take turns holding each stone briefly, they are encouraged to write whatever might come into their awareness onto the paper as a message for the stone's owner. Be open to whatever comes up. After everyone has written something on the paper for every stone, the original owner collects their stone and the messages written for them. As a group, discuss the intuitive perceptions and how they may accurately reflect or coincide with reality.

Intuitive Touch: Pair up with a partner. Sit facing each other, touching palms with right palm up, left palm down for approximately two minutes. Pay attention to any thoughts, words, images or physical sensations that come up during this time. Take a few moments to jot down the insights gathered, so that you might share them with your partner. How did each of you do?

Jewelry Intuition: Gather a metallic ring, watch or other jewelry item worn regularly by each participant. Place these items together in the center of the table, without identifying ownership. You might choose to place the items under a cloth to eliminate visual identification. Take turns holding each item and jot down any thoughts, emotions, words or images that come to mind as you hold it. Jot down a few notes and have players take turns sharing their perceptions.

4. Write down questions or decisions you need help with. Set a timer, close your eyes and focus on your breath for 10 minutes. Notice all the ideas, words and images that come into your mind. Witness it all, but don't judge. When the timer rings, write down the details you recall, even if some may seem crazy. Seek wisdom

within the details. Test what you learned for action using the tongue testing technique in number two.

5. Write down a question before you go to bed at night and set the intention that you are seeking an answer. Immediately upon waking jot down whatever you remember from your dreams. Make notes of people, places, animals, events, objects and strong feelings. What could these mean as metaphors related to your answer?

You'll never really know the true extent of your intuitive power unless you dare to use it. Just as weight lifting develops strong muscles, practice develops intuitive confidence. Don't beat yourself up if you miss 100 percent accuracy. Instead, be curious as you go forward. If you find you are more intuitive when it comes to other people but still feel blocked about your own messages, connect with friends who value intuition and exercise your intuitive muscles together playfully. Keep track of your intuitive hits in your journal and celebrate your development as you go.

Serving the Highest Purpose

In business school most people learn the phrase "highest and best use" in a discussion of investment. Highest and best use refers to making choices about where to invest money, people or resources so that you get the greatest return on investment. It also applies to how we live our lives and spend our precious time.

If you have a free hour available, is your highest and best use to spend it going to a networking event, scheduling a client session or taking a nap? The answer can be complicated. If you need to generate new business connections, want to get out of the office for a break, or just want to see people, the networking event might be the best choice. However, if a client really needs help or you've promised an appointment at a specific time, you must serve the client because that's an honorable way to spend that hour. If you happen to feel ill or totally exhausted, a nap may be a worthy option.

When it comes to the question about highest service, ask yourself, "What would love do?" When love gets thrown into the mix, it becomes bigger than money and time. *It becomes more about making a difference, helping someone or enjoying the process in the midst of the action,*

100

too. Sometimes things must be done because we've made a promise or commitment. That's certainly true for love, too. You might ask, "What does cleaning my bathroom have to do with love?" I would respond that if you love your home and the places in your home that help maintain your comfort and serve your daily needs, you might just want to show that love for your bathroom back by cleaning it to a glistening luster.

If you approach every choice from that perspective, you will smile as you get the job done. Put on a favorite song while you clean and there's more love for you to enjoy. Get it? I hope you do. Highest and best use plus love is an important lesson that really does help you shine and succeed at whatever you choose to be and do.

You can have more. You can have it all. Define what you want and seek it. Go after it. Slender, young, intuitive, glowing, it's all within your reach. Enjoy it.

Practice Time

1. Take your waist hip ratio measurement and record your measurement here.

_____ divided by _____ = _____
Waist (inches)   Hip (inches)   Waist-Hip Ratio

2. Refer to the 10 tips for Waist Management.

List the three tips you would find easiest to try.

a. _____

b. _____

c. _____

List the three tips for Waist Management that you would find most difficult or have no interest in trying.

a. _____

b. _____

c. _____

What do your selections tell you? Use EFT tapping on one specific item to acknowledge your resistance to change. See Appendix III for sample EFT treatment scripts.

3. Write a list of 20 things that make you laugh. Set the intention to laugh more.

4. How would having a greater sense of intuition be helpful to you? Write a paragraph about it in your journal.

Chapter 6

Invite Deeper Connection

"To get the full value of joy you must have somebody to divide it with."
Mark Twain

Stop Swimming in the Baby Pool

There's a phrase I hear almost every day in business that drives me crazy. *"Take it to the next level."* Those words hit me like nails on a chalk board because while I know people want to move to the next level, I also know that they are having an incredibly hard time actually getting there. If you really want to make progress I invite you to stop swimming in the shallow end of the baby pool and consider the possibility of deeper connections, more meaningful, deeper relationships that are firmly rooted in the foundation of love.

What do I mean by this? I mean that we need to take chances to connect with people, and more fully connect ourselves with the environment around us. We must be both vulnerable and proactive about going deep. Deeper connection means revealing ourselves authentically, offering validation and accepting love from others. For many people going deeper is just so scary. It offers the possibility of so much, yet it also offers the opportunity for rejection. Acknowledging that there are risks involved, allow me to help you go deeper with safety and greater confidence.

Who is Your Best Friend?

Your chance for finding the deepest connection begins with you—connecting with yourself, loving yourself and seeing the Divine being that is you. This can be the hardest part. Why is it so hard? Because we know all our imperfections, flaws, and mistakes. We scrutinize ourselves so closely that we focus mostly on the negative instead of the positive. Why not just accept the complete self, including all of those imperfections, unique talents, gifts, faults and failures so that you can move on and be yourself? It is hard, isn't it?

I want to remind you that you are a unique filter through which life is observed and expressed. You are an important piece of a giant puzzle and part of a Divine plan. God doesn't make mistakes. The things that you think are flaws are actually aspects that help connect you to the world around you. Because there are others who resonate with those talents, interests, flaws or imperfections, you will be drawn to one another. If you are someone who has overcome pain or who has been able to overcome a challenge, there will be many who will be helped by the lessons you have learned. Although you're not perfect, you have information, wisdom, kindness and compassion to help others. That's where your unique filter and your unique nature come into play.

You are under an agreement, a mission, to be yourself and to connect. To accomplish your mission, whether you like it or not, you're required to go deep. You are being asked to expand into places where you'll become excited, awed, inspired, enthused and awed again. You need not completely understand your mission right now, but I invite you to begin feeling it. That is part of being your own best friend. Understand what excites you. Understand what makes you feel whole and complete. Understand those moments where you are so connected to the world around you, and use these as clues to begin loving who you are.

There was a time many years ago when I found self-care and self-love to be almost impossible. I remember serving many masters during that time. As a mother of two small toddlers, I always felt guilty because I was working a full-time job. I was away from them more than I wanted to be, yet when I was finally home with them, I was so stressed and worn out that I couldn't enjoy the present moment. I was skimping on self-care and blaming myself for everything that went wrong. I was striving for perfection in all ways at all times, trying to be perfect at work, home and anywhere else I could find a place to be perfect.

It was exhausting, depleting and a game I could never win. And you know what? It really wasn't about loving myself. It was more about picking myself apart. I'm so glad that stopped, but it took plenty of pain, distress and tension before I surrendered and recognized the beleaguered state I was in. Maybe you understand that, too. Those were days when so many simple joys were missing and I failed to take the time to see what was missing.

Now I know what was missing, and it's not missing anymore. I WAS MISSING! I've found a way to come back into life, to connect with it, to go deep and to be who I am. Yes, I still have days when I deny my Divine nature and get stuck on some small detail of imperfection that slows me down. On the other hand, I'm able to identify those moments more quickly, witness them for what they are, back off and choose something better.

Emotional freedom techniques, or EFT, is an exceptional tool for nurturing self-love. EFT is a conscious way to cancel out negative thoughts that creep into your awareness allowing you to love yourself just as you are now. You cannot heal what you don't acknowledge and you cannot heal what you do not accept. So before any healing can happen, you've got to be aware of your thoughts. Accept them, acknowledge them, and then make your conscious choice. By choosing to love and forgive yourself, your energy field will expand and strengthen, automatically opening the door to deeper connection with all of creation. Your writing, voice, emails, influence, presence and all that you are will travel out more purely in all directions. Think of it like fishing with a bigger net. You now have a much greater capacity for catching what you want. Others will step closer as they notice the invisible positive signals you send. You will become like a beacon to their soul and the magnetic force of attraction will also draw you closer to those that you need to connect with.

The challenge now becomes going even deeper once those connections begin so that you can figure out what you will create together. Your divine nature includes loving yourself; sending the energy outward and being ready and willing to go deeper.

Honor Your Connection to Nature

Now that you're aware of developing self-love, another powerful tool that you can easily put into place is deeper connection with your physical surroundings, especially nature, including creatures, pets and the earth itself. There are so many ways to connect with nature and, as I've already stated earlier in this book, we are uniquely created to be connected to our natural world and to be thriving in this world that's been created to support us.

The problem with modern life and modern technology is that it seems to be pulling us farther and farther away from that beautiful natural setting that we were designed to be in. We've got to stop and come back to our natural roots. There are so many ways to do it. That's what makes me excited. I need to remind you of it, though, because this is a powerful way to nurture those deeper connections that really help you thrive.

Nature is all around us, even if you live in the suburbs or a big city. The outdoors is accessible through gardens, plants, animals, observing nature through a window, walking outdoors, breathing in fresh air, and gazing up at stars in the night sky. You can access nature with a bird feeder, watching branches blow in the breeze, observing the passing of seasons, or sitting by the shore watching the waves and tides change.

You can connect with nature wherever you are. Live plants can become part of your office or home décor. Photos or images of natural settings can bring nature to you. Perhaps easiest and most important, mindfully place your feet flat on the ground and set the intention that you are connected to the earth. Imagine that you can release what you don't need in terms of your negative energy right down into the earth.

I love taking time to ground frequently during the day. Think of your body just like the grounding end of a lightning rod. When the lightning strikes, where does the energy go? It gets absorbed into the earth. When you're full of tension and stress and the world around you isn't quite working for you, let that heavy, negative energy that isn't supportive of your wholeness to go right down into the earth. I notice the movement of energy down through my legs quite often when I'm working with clients during sessions, and it is comforting to know that the earth is there to absorb and transform the "yucky" stuff.

Why not get your feet flat on the floor right now? Take a few deep breaths, and as you exhale, set the intention that you're sending that heavy, unhealthy energy down into the earth. Set the intention that you're balancing your energy by sending the part that you don't need to the earth, knowing that earth can absorb it like a sponge. It's safe and easy for you to release when you are grounded.

Pets as Connectors and Teachers

Anybody who has owned a pet, either now or in the past knows that pets are a source of joy, humor, unconditional love, happy greetings, touch, and grounding power. They give us a chance to be responsible for the life of another creature, and they become part of our journey, no matter what life brings. I've personally had pets involved in my life for as long as I remember. Having a dog, cat and bird in my house offers beautiful sounds, soft fur, purring, wet kisses, cuddly moments and also a powerful force to help me get grounded. Those lovely four-legged creatures have mastered grounding so well. If you need to ground quickly, just touch your pet and it happens instantly.

A Story of Two Dogs: Grace after Loss

In early 2005, I was working long hours managing a group medical practice. Unhappy, depleted and confused, I felt compelled to speak with Valerie Stultz, a trusted friend and minister at a local Methodist church. I had been called to be a "spiritual leader" and wondered if ministry was something I should consider. Valerie had left her career as a teacher to attend seminary in her forties. She was the confidante and expert I needed to connect with.

When Pastor Valerie and I met on January 17, 2005, I came to realize that it was time to quit my job and pursue a new direction for my life. Not knowing exactly what I'd do next, I concluded that meeting knowing I would submit my resignation, then work for another 30 days to train my successor and tie up loose ends at the office. At the end of those 30 days I would rest, clear my mind and restore my spirit by taking at least a month off to do something productive yet mindless like painting baseboards.

Coincidentally, but not in my awareness, on that same day I reached my decision in Pastor Valerie's office, a tiny golden retriever puppy was born not far away.

The month following my resignation was busy and emotional. As my final week on the job arrived, much had been accomplished and the office was ready to operate without me. As I collapsed in bed, with just three more office days remaining, I was more than exhausted and ready for some time off. Suddenly around 1 a.m., I awakened with a start, realizing that my husband was not in the bed, and that all the lights were on downstairs. That was out of the ordinary. I got out of bed and went out to the hallway to see what was going on. There I saw my husband kneeling over our dog Kelly. I asked, "What's the matter?" He replied, "Come down here. This isn't good."

I rushed down the stairs and the minute I touched the dog I immediately knew something was seriously wrong. Kelly was cold as ice and barely breathing. Our four-year-old golden retriever had been fine just a few hours earlier, but now appeared to be close to death. We called the emergency clinic and whisked her off into the car without awakening our children. Dan and Mandy were old enough to be home alone and it seemed right at the time to let them sleep.

When we arrived at the clinic, the mystery continued. The vet was puzzled by her cool temperature and suspected there might be internal bleeding. Kelly was given an IV of warm fluids while we waited on the cold, hard benches for what seemed to be hours and hours.

At sunrise we were summoned to the exam room. Kelly had stabilized thanks to the warm fluids, but remained very ill. We were advised to transport her to a specialty clinic on the other side of town for additional tests. It was there, after many hours of waiting, that we received the information we didn't want to hear. An ultrasound revealed that Kelly had an inoperable tumor wrapped around her heart. We were offered two options: draining the excess fluid from the heart so we might bring her home for a few days or euthanize her to end the pain. I held Kelly, whispered goodbye and buried my face in her soft fur as she took her last breath. George and I left the clinic without our dear Kelly, in a state of total exhaustion. We braced ourselves for what we knew would be next—sharing the news with

Dan and Mandy as they arrived home from school. Although we had called to let them know we had taken Kelly to the vet, they had no idea what had happened. As they entered the house and saw our faces, they broke into tears. We held each other and cried. The emptiness, sadness and stillness in our home were palpable.

Suddenly something very painful occurred to me. In just two days I would be done with work, home alone during the day trying to get my act together without my precious companion, Kelly. The absence of daily walks, feeding times and four-legged footsteps on the floor were painful reminders of my loss. When I had originally thought about those 30 days of clearing my mind and painting baseboards, I had also imagined taking Kelly for walks and enjoying her company while the kids were in school. Suddenly the reality of my loss smacked so hard. Saying good-bye to my coworkers would compound my grief this week, too. I was angry at God. How could God let this happen when I had finally followed the call to become a spiritual leader?

The following Saturday morning, after a lonely week had passed, it suddenly occurred to me that there was a place in my heart for a new pet. Why hadn't I thought of this sooner? I had committed to spending these first 30 days of freedom at home, doing not much of anything. This gift of time offered me the perfect chance to train, house break and bond with a puppy. I thought to myself, "I wonder if this could work?"

I immediately pulled out the newspaper and I found an advertisement for eight golden retriever puppies just a few miles away. I called the number and headed out for a visit. I would be the very first person to take a look at this litter of puppies. Almost as soon as I entered that house, one puppy picked me. She was a confident auburn-coated female with huge paws. I was cautious. I tried not to bond with her and left that morning without making a commitment. My heart had been broken and somehow it was hard to open up to a new puppy when I knew I might one day lose her too.

I returned that afternoon with my husband and daughter. The deal was sealed when that puppy picked them, too. We returned home with a new family member and enormous grins on our faces. The healing had begun.

Appropriately, we named her Grace. We needed "grace" and this new energy came to heal my family at a time of loss and transition. What seemed to be an illogical betrayal soon proved to be a true gift as part of a larger plan. Grace was very intelligent, followed commands and bonded tightly with me during the month that followed. She was so different from Kelly, a hyper animal whom we had loved in spite of the fact that she had never followed our commands or developed appropriate manners for our visitors. Gracie was uniquely suited to be the companion to the healer I was ready to become.

Gracie is now six years old, my constant companion, receptionist and business partner. Gracie sleeps at my feet while I work. She doesn't seem to mind when I must ignore her. She's quiet and patient, knowing that I usually don't have time to walk or play during regular business hours. Gracie loves the clients and groups who come for sessions at my office. She has a way of making every visitor feel welcome. She especially likes leaning on their feet when they first arrive. "Leaning" is how she absorbs energy, grounds our visitors and gets to know them. She respectfully interacts with each person depending on how they're interacting with her. Gracie is a healer who contributes to client sessions in sensitive and sometimes humorous ways. She has a knack for helping people feel good in her presence.

Grace has given me so many regular opportunities to laugh, play and connect with nature, friends and strangers too. Sometimes you'll hear her barking in my audios and you'll see her gently interrupt me in my videos. One of her most precious interruptions is on my film "Get Grounded." You can view it at www.energymakeover4U.com

I hope you, too, will open your heart to God's grace through a pet. Yes, you may outlive your pet and ultimately experience heartbreak, but the lessons of constant and unconditional love taught by our furry friends are a priceless blessing.

Seek Support

Who do you turn to for reliable and helpful connection? Could you be doing more of it? Everyone can build their energy reserves and abilities by having support systems in place. Support comes from people who care to be there for you, who are reliable, responsible, responsive, helpful, knowledgeable and understanding. Support people can help you do hard things. They will be there to accompany you through both good and bad times. They celebrate with you and they will be there to offer a shoulder and a tissue when times get rough.

Who's in Your Support System?

Take a moment to think about the people in your life. You've got family, friends, neighbors, coworkers, suppliers, contractors and clients too. Perhaps you also have people you network with for your business, people you admire and respect as well as people you know through social networking online. Hopefully, you also have a few mentors. There is support everywhere. Take a moment to get in touch with the support system you already have and allow yourself to feel gratitude and appreciation for that. Begin to consider how you might deepen these valuable connections.

Have you been holding back? Are there people who could move from being basic acquaintances to real friends? Where might you find deeper, safer, and more reliable connections? Set an intention that you want deeper connection, and don't hold back. You are safe when you go deep with loving intentions. Ask for what you need as you also find clarity on what you bring to each relationship.

A support system that has been there for me over the last 20 years has been Weight Watchers. I have been a lifetime member of Weight Watcher's since 1991 and can't say enough about the incredible support they have given me through regular meetings, friends with common values, recipes, new ideas and support for both the good and the bad times. I like that I can count on them for structure, meeting my needs and inspiring leadership at meetings. I appreciate that they have helped me develop really positive habits, yet keep me growing with program innovation and a constant flow of new resources. I give back by encouraging new members and by sharing tips and stories at meetings. We are all better off because we came together and revealed ourselves to each other.

When I started my business, I wanted to create support for women in my community. Many business networking groups existed around town, but I noticed these were lacking the elements of natural health, personal growth, and spiritual development. I decided that I would create a group that would merge networking, educational topics, energy self-care and a positive message. This monthly breakfast group, The Indigo Connection, has been meeting for six years and it has been a thrill to have provided a place where professional women can foster deeper connections.

The Indigo Connection also holds several retreats each year where women come together for extended times of rest, reflection and healing. I urge the women to let their hearts open, be themselves, share ideas and grow in the midst of complete safety and acceptance. We create quite a few miracles in the space of just a few days. If this sounds appealing to you, additional retreats and events are planned and you are invited to learn more by joining my mailing list at www.energy-makeover4u.com. Consider becoming one of our business affiliates by starting an Energy Makeover® group in your community.

Cruising with Like Minds

In 2008 I took a writing seminar as part of an extraordinary seven-day ocean cruise, involving some of the world's most outstanding personal growth leaders including Wayne Dyer, Sylvia Browne, Cheryl Richardson, Brian Weiss, Doreen Virtue, Maryanne Williamson and Carolyn Myss. This was a charter voyage organized by Hay House Publishing, which meant that just about every person on board was of like mind.

The energy on this voyage was certainly different from any other cruise I had ever taken. This kind of experience makes me keenly aware of how people we choose to spend time with can affect our experience. Spending time with people who share our values and see the world in a similar way allows us relax and be ourselves. Like-minded people are less likely to drain your energy and are far more likely to give you the means to build it up. Certainly a cruise experience is an ideal setting; nevertheless it demonstrates how good it can be.

Your Challenge

The challenge I pose now is that you take a little time to review the key relationships in your life. Do you share something positive in common with these important people in your life? Have you ever taken time to find out where the other person is coming from? Think about your partner, coworkers, family members, friends and acquaintances. Consider the following questions:

1. What do you hold as truth in your life? How does your version of truth compare with that of the people you spend so much time with?

2. Do you share your beliefs openly with people in your life? Do you feel you can without being attacked or judged?

3. Do you allow other people to share what they believe without judgment or interruption?

4. When you disagree with others, how do you communicate your difference of opinion?

5. When other people disagree with you, how do you react? Do you speak out, stay quiet or change the subject?

Finding a friend of like mind is an amazing way to build energy and gain the courage to follow your heart through even the most difficult times. Even if you're not sure what you believe, there is someone out there feeling the same way. We were meant to connect and share. We can certainly learn through the experiences of other people and can teach through our own sharing. We can feel safer and more secure in the presence of like minds.

Simply being present as an open-minded witness can be one of the most healing things you can do, whether you agree with them or not. When you allow yourself to simply be open, present and listening, a space is created for hearts to connect. Pay attention to your relationships this week and celebrate the healing power of a kindred, supported spirit:

- Be the first person to reach out.
- Initiate conversation.
- Ask for an opinion.
- Say something to honor the spirit of another.
- Be careful about judgment.

- Honor the honesty someone else expresses.
- Find the common ground, then dig deeper from there.

All you need to do is be open and receptive. If you find you share deep values and love the same things, earth becomes just a bit more like heaven. You have created a space where it is safe to be you, and you've given your friend permission to join you there, exactly as they are.

Serve What You Love

"To serve is beautiful, but only if it is done with joy and a whole heart."
Pearl S. Buck

Are you 100 percent in touch with what you love? Could you re-cite 100 things you love off the top of your head? Would doing so bring you a silly grin and a skip in your step? How does what you love translate into a magical force in your daily life? If you really want to harness the power of deep connection, know what you love, find it, serve it and be it.

There are many ways to do and be what you love. The inhabitants of this world are waiting for you to volunteer, teach, read, post comments, contribute, reach out, write, share and gather others around a cause. Whether you do it for pay or do it because you care, serving what you love will be one of the easiest things you can choose to do.

Deeper Conversations

If you want to engage in really deep connection and be interesting and interested, one of the best ways to do that is to get clear about what you love and what others really love, too. If you and your spouse or best friend each put together a list of 100 things you love about being alive, I suspect you would learn something new that you didn't know before. This can happen even if you've known this person for decades, giving you new clues for how to connect even more deeply with special people.

Your job as a connector is to find that passion in another person that lies dormant, unexpressed or hidden by fear of judgment. By help-ing another person discover their love for life, you enrich the planet and awaken connection. It is astounding to see the world through the eyes and heart of another person. Even if you read the same book, see the same show or watch the same movie you'll each have a unique response to it. Nobody's right or wrong. You each have access to a different angle on the truth.

Develop respect for diversity and learn that ideas outside of your own have merit and are worthy of consideration. Start the deeper conversations and have fun as the doors open.

Viewing Situations from God's Perspective

I remember observing the posts of two respected friends on Facebook that allowed me to see how people coming from two different angles were actually able to come together. One of these friends, "Jack," is a vegan, often posting about the beauty of the vegan lifestyle. He's extremely passionate because his personal experience as a vegan has been so healthy and positive. Another one of my Facebook friends, "Beth," is a nutritional expert who helps people who have eating disorders. She's passionate about making sure people are healthy, nutritionally balanced and emotionally sound. She sees restrictive diets and being vegan in a very different way.

When these two friends came together in a debate over a post about nutrition, I saw each of them awaken the other to a new perspective without being judgmental. Consciously they both agreed that there was truth coming from the other perspective, then apologized for being insensitive to the other position. They suddenly became aware of a wider array of options within a position. Jack and Beth came together, appreciating that there were extremes in their way of seeing the world, but also valued the opinion of the other person. As each stepped aside to see the situation through the other person's eyes, they gained a valid perspective. God surely sees things from every perspective. As we connect with our Source, we can do this too. Look for a new angle and try to see it as God sees it so you might enjoy some deeper connections.

Marriage and Family

Being part of a family creates the foundation upon which all other relationships are built. I was lucky to have been born to parents who made it easy for me to believe I was lovable. For that I am truly grateful. I've learned through my short time as a personal coach that so many seemingly normal and strong individuals were not so lucky. Stories of physical and verbal abuse my clients have shared with me about the pain endured as children have brought me to tears. Betrayal and abuse within marriage is also far too common in the lives of my coaching clients. My heart aches for all of them more often than I would like, yet it is part of the reality that makes Energy Makeover® necessary and relevant.

How do you heal the pain connected to those very deep connections? Marriage and family should be a source of energy enrichment. What action is necessary when deep connections are painful? It is in those times when we must address forgiveness. Forgiveness encompasses asking for forgiveness, forgiving others and loving the one who has hurt you from a distance, if that's necessary. Forgiveness is not just a mental exercise. In order to be completely free, energetic release is also required.

Emotional Freedom Techniques (EFT) and heart massage are two excellent methods that I use regularly with clients to facilitate forgiveness. You can proactively use these techniques before family gatherings to bring yourself into these situations in a more peaceful and balanced state. In Appendix III, you will find a self-care treatment script for forgiveness. I invite you to see situations where forgiveness would be appropriate, acknowledge that there's something to release, accept it and choose to let it go.

Energetic healing methods are incredible ways to forgive, not just in your head but deep into your heart. Clean up your energy so that your signal is pure and undiluted with the negative disruptions you hold on to. Make a choice to forgive and you will be free.

Soul Mates, Romance and Marriage

My marriage has been a source of strength, joy and deep connection for me. George, my husband of 27 years, is my best friend and someone who is always there to support me. We fortunately share a wide range of values and priorities, keep our minds open, and respect our differences, too. Respect really is the key to our happiness. He may watch way too much British soccer on TV (in my opinion) but I am okay with that because I know he loves it. We are different but can co-exist peacefully. We give each other space, but also know that we can speak up and ask for what we need. Usually those requests receive a "yes," and love reigns above our need to control each other.

I believe that we connect with romantic partners through a process of soul recognition and the mission we choose. I remember the specific moment back in college when a spark ignited between the two of us. It happened unexpectedly as I met his gaze in a different way for the first time. It was as if I was hit by a two-by-four and suddenly realized "This is somebody I need to remember."

In Michael Newton's book, Destiny of Souls, regression case studies cited suggest that significant moments in the life you are about to live are shown to you before you incarnate. I truly believe that the moment I met George and saw him in this electrified way for the first time was something that was embedded in my soul. It was shown to me ahead of time as a moment I needed to pay attention to. I didn't let go of it. The years after that moment were hard for us. We were separated for over five years, living in two different cities. Finishing college degrees while separated a long distance apart from one another added to our challenges. It seemed impossible that we could plan to make a life together when we were only able to see each other once or twice a year. Something about that spark kept us working in the same direction even in the midst of challenges.

I share this with you because there are opportunities for your deep relationships when you recognize that spark of insight. You might actually feel a jolt or a spark within you accompanied by a physical sensation in your heart. If you feel a mysterious soul connection, even if you don't understand it, pay attention and act upon it. Don't be scared. Remember that you feel this spark because it is offering you an opportunity to be the person you chose to be.

You always have choice and the ability to test your hunches. You might want to go slowly at first. Know that there's energy there to help you properly connect with the right, deeper connections. Everybody deserves at least one special friend in their lives. That kind of person is out there for you, too. Demand depth and support, and be willing to give it. Renew your vows of marriage and renegotiate how you want your relationship to be. Be open to compromise and if necessary allow trained counselors to guide you in conversation into that deeper place of respect and connection.

Both parties can get what they need to thrive and grow, once those needs get out on the table. Express yourself: ask for what you want and be willing to give in recognition that the other person has valid needs as well.

Parenthood

Parenthood is a complicated and very deep connection. Becoming a mother opened the door to two of the deepest, most complicated human relationships I ever imagined. I knew that having children was an important dream even at a young age. Somehow I think motherhood was one of the main themes in the life purpose that I crafted for myself. Parenthood is a role that teaches you about fears, dreams, balance, trust, and most importantly love. Back in 2005 as I was just beginning to develop my coaching practice, I attended a weekend seminar in Calgary, Alberta called "Power of Focus for Women," facilitated by Fran Hewitt, wife of Les Hewitt, co-author of one of my favorite books, *The Power of Focus.*

This seminar was designed as a weekend of deep introspection, learning and growth. The experience raised a new uneasiness about my role as a mother, as I found myself questioning the decisions I had made throughout my life. I wondered if I had let my children down, particularly because I chose to continue with my career after they were born.

During my long flight home, I wrote each of my children a letter asking them to forgive me for any way I had short-changed them. I also asked each of them how I could improve at my important role as their mother. My words expressed hope that I had done enough to help them be kind, independent and successful people. Putting those words on paper seemed to lift a huge burden from my heart.

After I distributed the letters to Dan and Mandy, their responses were surprisingly nonchalant. My daughter, Mandy,14 at the time, told me that she always liked attending daycare and that she felt stronger and more independent than most of her peers because of it.

Dan, then 17, responded quietly saying that there was no need to apologize. He thanked me for a life that was so good. I was a bit mystified and also relieved. How had I conjured up so much angst when it never even existed?

Today I look upon my adult son and daughter and see abundant evidence that my role as a parent resulted in success. My son has completed college, has a good job and many meaningful friendships. My daughter is entering her third year of college with good grades, excellent social connections and a steady boyfriend who treats her with respect. Dan and Mandy are managing life in the "real world" admirably, as good people with values reflecting mine, including health, honesty, fitness, compassion, humor, relationships, family and career.

I've heard it said that a mother's anxiety never goes away. My kids will always be my babies. I will worry if they are late or I don't hear from them when I expect to. Being a mother involves love, trust and letting go, yet we continue to hold onto them tightly. I remember how my anxiety would melt away on those days so long ago when they snuggled on my lap. Now my comfort comes from watching them take flight with life and responsibility. The nest may be empty but the bonds remain strong.

Becoming a Vulnerable Leader

One of the best ways to have a powerful and deeper connection to the world around you is to become a leader. Leaders have to take charge and help others accomplish things. Leaders lead causes, motivate, inspire, facilitate change and help other people's voices be heard.

Consider the possibility of choosing to be a *vulnerable leader*—someone so strong they can expose their tender heart, leaving it wide open. Imagine being so honest, passionate, confident and focused that you put yourself out there, completely vulnerable to attack and criticism, yet remain strong and protected by a powerful and resilient energy state that you're easily able to hold. That energy comes from a deep connection to love.

To be able to show your vulnerability as a leader is an exquisite power that the world especially needs now. Resolve to get out of the shallow end and instead be a serious contender who connects, initiates, leads, energizes, loves and serves. Use what you love to inspire that kind of inner strength. An open-hearted loving connection to every relationship will manifest massive results in the end. Don't cheat yourself. Just do it.

I hadn't generally paid much attention to political rhetoric until the last presidential campaign when I witnessed something that was quite refreshing—a candidate who took the chance to be vulnerable in the public eye. That candidate, Hillary Clinton, admitted that she was worried about how hard it was to be involved in politics, speaking from the heart as cameras were rolling as her voice choked and tears filled her eyes. Looking back, I admire what she revealed that day. She showed us that she's human, vulnerable and passionate about the difficult choices she's made in her decision to become a leader. Some might say that this was just another political stunt full of positioning and theatrics. I firmly beg to differ. As someone who reads the energy behind communication, her words, voice and most importantly the place where the energy came from, the heart, told me that she was letting her guard down to expose the truth.

In that unscripted moment, I heard her voice soften and saw her eyes well up. Her words came straight from the heart. I wonder if at that moment she suddenly found herself worrying that she had made an impulsive and deadly political error. She took a chance, speaking out of her heart without a script, and showing the world a weaker more vulnerable side. Would she be rejected for it?

We all know that Hillary didn't end up becoming the President. We also know that she was appointed to a very important position to lead diplomatic relations as Secretary of State. I believe she's ideally suited for that important role. Women are peace makers, more inclined to show that vulnerable, yet powerful, side.

Being vulnerable is letting your guard down, opening your heart and being true to yourself in word, act and thought. Being vulnerable in its best sense allows the human side to shine through, and a deep, solid connection to be made with others. It doesn't apply only to leaders. That same power can come through when you are in any position of influence, whether it is as a speaker, a trainer, a manager, spouse, friend or parent.

120

Being vulnerable is risky. What if people don't like what they see and hear? The fact of the matter is you're sharing deep truth. Truth from your heart. Putting that true self out there and being criticized or attacked is so scary that most people never do it. Only the incredibly strong ones do. They are the ones who truly love and accept themselves.

Will you decide to be one of the strong ones and do it anyway? I sincerely hope you do. I will always be attracted to the vulnerable leader, the one who uses that heart energy to send pure messages that open the door to deep connection. God bless the vulnerable leader. Be one and watch your connections deepen.

Practice Time

1. Choose something you will do today to nurture a greater love for yourself. Jot down a few sentences about this commitment each day in your journal.

2. Find a way to bring more nature into your daily life. List three ways you could easily do it that you can begin today.

3. Write a story about an animal that has had a positive influence on your life.

4. Take a 60-second grounding break. Do this by getting your feet flat on the floor, closing your eyes and beginning to breathe. As you breathe in, take in a positive thought or a thought of gratitude. As you exhale, imagine letting go what you no longer need and sending it into the earth through the soles of your feet. Inhaling in gratitude, exhaling the release of toxic patterns and thoughts. Do this for 60 seconds and then resume whatever productive activity you had going on.

5. List 10 people you spend the most time with. On this list, identify the following. Which ones are:

   • Like minds
   • Support systems
   • Energy vampires
   • Prospects for deeper connection

   People can be placed in more than one category. Use this awareness as you engage in setting priorities for those deeper connections in your life.

6. Who do you need to forgive? Make a list. Pick one of these situations or people on the list and use the EFT for Forgiveness script in Appendix III to release the bonds that hold you entangled to this situation. Let it go and move on.

7. How can you become a vulnerable yet stronger leader? Jot down a few ideas and take these thoughts into a conversation with someone you've identified for deeper connection.

Chapter 7

Escape to Magical Places

"Climb the mountains and get their good tidings. Nature's peace will flow into you as sunshine flows into trees. The winds will blow their own freshness into you, and the storms their energy, while cares will drop off like autumn leaves."
John Muir

I remember a time in early 2005 when I hit the wall, a term runners use to describe the sudden fatigue that hits so solidly that it makes it impossible to take another step. In my case, when this happened I realized that I was so worn out that I needed to quit my job. I needed an extreme escape, but I didn't have the energy to plan anything elaborate. All I could come up with at that time was the promise to spend the next 30 days sleeping in, painting baseboards (the most mundane yet productive task I could think of), and trying to find out what was left of worn-out me.

I was smart enough then to know I needed to be in better form if I was to be inspired and guided to a better way of being. I survived the rough spell and found some new tools to help me thrive. Today I run on a steady stream of high energy that allows me to be a leader in helping others heal, have fun and connect more fully to the world around them.

Healthy escapes are fundamental pieces of the Energy Makeover® tool kit, for keeping the energy and personal comfort equation in balance. In my experience, escapes offer opportunities for enormous jumps in consciousness, huge jolts of joy and a massive recharge of the spirit. Whether you want to call them daydreams, retreats, getaways, vacations, artist dates or romantic weekends, they offer support, structure, environment and inspiration for transformation. They build gratitude and also allow self-discovery.

There is additional magic when groups gather for supportive getaways. Studies show that women build their levels of the well-being hormone oxytocin when they gather for friendship and support. Ladies, imagine what a weekend or full week with your girlfriends could do for you! I assure the husbands and boyfriends out there that women come back from these getaways ready to be more receptive to you, too. Everybody wins.

When planning your escape, make sure whatever you choose supports you in building energy around something you love. Leave the distractions behind. In today's world that means setting some boundaries before you go, which can include turning off your cell phone, letting others know you are out of reach for a few hours or even days. Getaways that involve excessive sleep deprivation, hangovers, gambling and credit card debt are not likely to bring the healing recovery you had in mind. Be careful about your choices and use the following questions to guide you in brainstorming some suitable getaway options.

Who?

Do I need time alone? Is it time to connect with a special friend or a group? Does my marriage or romantic relationship need time for reconnection? Do I need to meet new people and create new friendships? Who would I choose as part of an escape, and why? Who can help me pull the details together? Who will manage things for me at home while I'm away?

What?

What kind of places and activities have I been dreaming of? What activity level do I seek? What kind of travel and accommodations can I afford? Will it be elaborate or something very simple? Will I choose a repeat of a pleasant experience from the past so that I know what I'm getting into?

When?

Will this happen within a week, month, this year or beyond? Do I have vacation time available for this escape? How long can I hope to be away? What season makes the most sense for what I want to do? Can the others I want to escape with get away when I'm free?

Where?

Is there a particular place offering experiences and the environment to meet my needs? Am I seeking sun, warmth, water, mountains, snow, nature, entertainment, shopping, history, sacred sites, learning or physical activity? What are some perfect places that are easy to reach in a short time? Is there someplace you've dreamed of that has not yet become a reality?

Why?

This may be the most important part, so give it full consideration. Examine your intentions carefully. Why do you need this escape? How do you want to feel when it's over? How will you know you've accomplished what you intended by taking this break? And just in case you were wondering, I have many suggestions for getaways of all sizes. They are included at the end of this chapter.

Make Escape a Priority

Many people, especially workaholics, find it hard to see how an escape contributes to increased productivity, success or happiness. Unless you make escape a priority it just won't happen. Your escape time will keep getting pushed to the back burner for someday or later.

Wake up and put yourself and your energetic health first. Escape is the way to recharge your energy battery and fire up your power to manifest even more in the physical world. Escape has been proven to increase health and longevity[*], too, so that's one more reason to take it seriously.

If money is the issue, start a savings fund today as you begin daydreaming and doing your research. This allows you to begin the escape from your chair at home. This need not be a struggle. Much of my joy as a world traveler has come from the planning process before the trip. That can be your priority, even if the trip must take place later for budgetary reasons.

---

[*] B.B. Gump and K.A. Matthews, "Are vacations good for your health? The 9-year mortality experience after the multiple risk factor intervention trial." *Psychosom Med.* 62(5) (September-October 2000): 608-12.

By setting plans in motion you are creating a strong, positive energy field to attract the experience into your reality. Once this begins, you may find exceptional bargains for the exact experiences you desire suddenly becoming available to you. Watch for synchronicity!

Daydreams: Your Thoughts Running Wild

I remember watching an interview in 2009 with Michael, Phelps, that incredible Olympic swimmer. He had just won his seventh gold medal, putting him in a tie with Mark Spitz for the most gold medals ever won by an athlete. He still had an opportunity to beat that, eventually returning with eight gold medals.

As the interview was wrapping up, Bob Costas asked Michael for any last words he wanted to share. Michael expressed his belief that having the imagination to believe something amazing was possible was the key to his winning experience. Imagination allowed him to *feel it happening* long before it ever became reality. Michael Phelps had already experienced winning in his imagination, in his mind and in his heart.

Daydreams and imagination are exactly how the law of attraction works. We don't have to be perfect at it. We simply need to imagine a view or a situation in our own version of perfection. Positive imagination is a process that feels good, and it offers healing potential. Setting aside doubts and fears for a brief time while focusing on a lively picture of success is something that engages a magnetic force. The more vivid this image can become, the more we can attract this experience to the physical domain. This is exactly what Michael Phelps described he could do.

Allow yourself daily moments to daydream and create exciting images and feelings in your mind. Use your heart to connect deeply with what you focus on. If you feel a negative thought or a doubt coming into the image, notice it and then challenge your mind to create something better by saying,
"Wouldn't it be better if _____*"* (fill in the blank and repeat often)

Tapping the EFT points to a litany of, "Wouldn't it be better if..." statements can you're your spirit and even get you giggling. Try it with a group sometime as a way to generate positive daydreams together. It really works. Allow your daydreams to inspire your writing, your living surroundings, things you create and even your business. You'll wonder how this can be so easy yet produce such astounding results. It brings imagination to the real world. So don't discount the time you spend in your daydreams.

Magical Places at Home

Our homes are magical places and must be nurturing to our mind, body and spirit. You should be able to feel completely safe and comfortable at home. As you look around your house, are there ample reflections of what you love and value? If your home doesn't provide that, you have a huge opportunity for an Energy Makeover®.

Allow me to share the story of the Italy room in my home, and how I was inspired to create a space that opened up so many doors to my own healing. This room has also facilitated the healing of hundreds of other people. I never imagined that! When I traveled with my family to southern Italy in 2004, I found myself mesmerized by the warmth of the sun, the blue of the sky and the water, colorful pottery and the beauty of the fresh produce. I thought to myself, "How could this feeling be part of my life back in Cleveland in the middle of a frozen winter?" I thought long and hard about this while in Italy and upon returning home I decided to create a transformation of a single room.

My vision was to create an Italy room in my sunroom, just off my kitchen. Fortunately my husband was supportive of the idea. Thank goodness he loved it, because I needed some help to pull it off. We sponge-painted the vaulted ceiling a bright yellow and then painted the walls a glorious sky blue that reminded me of our visit to Positano on Italy's Amalfi Coast. We furnished the room with framed photos from our travels, bright sunflowers, live plants, a fountain, two comfortable, cushy recliners, a café table for two and some lovely Italian pottery pieces. I accomplished it all on a tiny budget, which was part of the thrill.

The room soon became a spectacular haven for us for reading and intimate dinners for two. Our project created so much joy and perpetuated the good feelings from our travel. Our vision to bring the Italian summer to a cold, January day in Cleveland was accomplished.

I often retreat to this room when I need a quiet place to journal or make important decisions. It was in this room that I composed my first business plan for The Indigo Connection. It was here that I wrote my morning pages during my first independent study of Julia Cameron's book *The Artist's Way*. The Italy room became my meditation place, where I practice my speaking, and still serves as my creative studio in every sense of the word.

Today that Italy room is often used for live coaching and healing sessions with my clients, although the space was created long before I ever imagined having my own energy healing practice. My love for this space, the peace it creates and how it facilitates the energetic connections that heal, was a deliberate, creative process that continues to serve me well.

How could you energize your office, home or other special place so that it resonates with you in the images, colors, feelings or memories that you love? This need not be a radical adjustment, simply an addition of a deliberately selected focal point or enhancement. Even subtle shifts can make a big difference. Consider what you might choose to discard or give away so that you can make room for something new that brings greater happiness to you.

Make Sure to Set a Healing Intention

Ask yourself how you would like to feel, be and function when in this special space. Write an affirmation statement that communicates this creative desire in present tense language. Here's the statement that I used before I created the Italy room:

"I have successfully created the experience of light, warmth and uplifted heart that feels just like summer in Italy. This energy restores the soul no matter what is going on outside. It is available to me and everyone who enters this space."

Over the years I've had the chance to notice that when clients truly open up to creativity they connect to their own power and healing soon follows. The healing I speak of can take many forms, including reduction of symptoms, better relationships, more confidence and greater joy in daily life. Creativity allows us to spread our wings and do new things. It allows us to stop trying to control the world and instead gain a sense of safety as we nurture ourselves in the moment and the space we're in.

Use your creative power to transform your life in ways that reflect what you value and what makes you happy. Know you deserve it and that it's possible. Enjoy knowing that as you create happiness for yourself you may just find yourself changing the world around you.

If you are going to take on a project at home or in your office, consider hiring a Feng Shui consultant to assist you with this process. Feng Shui consultants provide valuable tips to help improve energy flow in healthy ways and will find practical solutions to support your intentions for your space. If you live in northeast Ohio I highly recommend Feng Shui practitioner Cara Gallagher at CaraGallagher. com. You can access a directory of Feng Shui schools and practitioners at www.FengShuiDirectory.com.

I never suspected that honoring my own inner desire for creation of the Italy room would someday become a healing space for others, too. It manifested anyway. That was part of the miracle. You can create it, too.

Explore

Exploration of spaces and places, experiences and settings is necessary to broaden your ability to escape. Even in the midst of an actual escape, whether it is a retreat, getaway or family vacation, the act of exploring a special place is the magic. Guidebooks and websites can get you started with ideas, but each person explores differently. My best advice is to lace up your most comfortable shoes and take a long walk. Indulge your inner child as you explore new places. Use all of your senses as you see sights, meet people, sample local foods, view history, listen to music, shop the stores and experience natural beauty.

Capture your memories and observations through journaling, finding special mementos, writing poetry, creating art, and recording history with your camera lens. One of my favorite travel experts, Rick Steves (www.RickSteves.com) has enriched my European travel experiences by urging that we venture off the traditional tourist venues and mingle with the locals. His guidebooks are spot-on when it comes to safe, enjoyable and enriching experiences to satisfy a wide variety of escapes. I also highly recommend his organized tours for people who enjoy the convenience and efficiency of a tour that also allows for plenty of free time for individual exploration.

If I had never explored Italy as part of a Rick Steves tour I would have never considered recreating the feeling of Italy back at home. Thank you, Rick.

Natural Splendor

Some of the most awe-inspiring moments are those that take place amidst nature, at least it's that way for me. Many find their God and a connection to the presence of a Divine higher power through the magical link with nature. Are you inspired by sunrises, sunsets, crashing waves or beautiful flowers? Perhaps you find yourself stirred to attention by mountain peaks, rock formations, rivers, lakes and waterfalls. Maybe your eyes are drawn to the beauty of forests, birds and exotic animals as well.

Even if you don't like insects, heat, rain, ice, mud or heavy winds, you could probably quickly find a kind of natural setting that speaks most directly to your heart and allows you to be comfortable. If you've been to these special places before, consider returning. If you've only seen photos and dream of one day visiting in person, fill your world with these images and set the intention to see them in person. Make a point of honoring your love for nature by filling your home with natural images to remind you of the splendor that you love. As you create deeper connections with new friends, ask them to share their favorite natural splendors. Better yet, explore these splendors together.

Sacred Spaces and Places

We need not be worshipping in a cathedral, standing inside ancient Stonehenge, exploring the site of the great pyramid or overlooking a vista in Sedona, Arizona to consider ourselves in a sacred place. Sacred places like those I mentioned do exist and if you are an energy sensitive person like me you will come to appreciate the amazing energy they offer.

Please do not limit yourself by thinking that sacred energy is only found in certain places or in short supply. You can intentionally create it. One of the essential concepts that I practice and teach as a healing professional has to do with preparing the right environment or sacred space to contain the process at hand. Certainly, any purposeful gathering of people can improve considerably if you simply take a moment to be fully present and set the stage for what is to come. This applies to business meetings, classes, lectures, small groups, one-on-one sessions with clients and for your own self-care, meditation or prayer routine. It is a process of deliberate presence.

It is up to you to choose how you'll create a sacred place for your own miracles. I offer the following ideas for consideration. Pick one or several. Consider the context of your goals, the others involved and certainly be practical. There are many paths to the right answer. Go in with the intention of creating a space that builds rapport, creates safety and allows comfort.

1. **Clear the energy in the space.** Open a window, light a candle, burn incense, use essential oils with smudge, sage or sweet grass to clear the energy and prepare the space for healing work. Soft lighting, sounds, music, tones, chimes and voice can also be helpful in shifting the energy to a more healing nature. You can clear the energy by simply setting a clearing intention.

2. **Pause to breathe and become present to the space.** You might choose to place your palms over the heart, close your eyes and be fully in your body. Honor whatever you may feel and accept it as your present truth. Consider the power you bring to a meeting as you simply take a moment to breathe deeply before you jump into the agenda.

3. **Set intentions.** Ask to create a positive experience. Know what you want to do. In business we have agendas. In your Energy Makeover® you can also have an agenda, but consider it a soft one based on your intentions rather than a specific outcome.

4. **Connect with a higher power.** Invite a Divine presence to be with you. This can include your definition of God, divine mother, Jesus, archangels, angels, guides, power animals, universal life force energy or a healing symbol. Honor the beliefs of all involved with the intention of inclusion and a common connection.

5. **Anchor the space.** Many healers like to invoke a pyramid of light, anchored at each corner by a powerful archangel. Others may prefer to install a bubble of light. You may also choose to bring in an image of a special healing place that you carry in your heart. Think of this anchoring process as establishing an energetic container to safely hold the energy of what will occur in the space.

6. **Ask for resources.** As you create the perfect setting, open yourself to intuition, ideas, synchronicity and opportunity. Imagine that you are opening a door and all that you need is lining up to support you. What would you like to have access to if the answer was "yes"? Believe that a "yes" is there for you.

7. **Surrender and release.** Let go of what you can't control and what seems impossible. Say good-bye to the distractions, disappointments and those long standing battles with your tormentors. Be aware of what has drained you and give it up for healing and transformation.

8. **Affirm.** Begin to see what you desire as if it has already happened and already exists. This can be a bank balance, a published book, a vacation, an important decision, a partner or a physical miracle of your choosing. Create words of affirmation. Express gratitude and accept the energy of the blessing you are creating in your mind.

9. **Engage in the work.** Whether it is a healing intervention with a group, a client or simply your own self-care session, your preparation of the space helps each individual engage more fully. Healing will have been initiated before you actually begin the work, by preparing the space.

10. **Close with gratitude and reverence.** Be thankful for the time and resources that came together in the space as well as the healing that occurred. Remain hopeful about those things that are not yet complete. Sometimes healing takes a while. Appreciate the experience and the space for what it was and what it provided.

Retreats and Getaways

I have personally found that removing myself from my routines and giving myself some time and space to enjoy quiet moments in beautiful places has a way of opening up my creative flow resulting in the highest and best version of me. I learned this early in life from my parents, Clyde and Gail Bartter. Mom loved a slow stroll in the woods for the simple joy of identifying plants and watching birds. Dad adored fishing in lakes, ponds and streams for hours, even when nothing was biting. These quiet places and open spaces made way for insights, intuitive guidance and a nice slice of peace. Give yourself this peaceful gift and the whole planet shifts in a good way. Imagine what would happen if more of us did it more often!

Over the years I've enjoyed countless getaways with girl scouts, summer camps, church retreats, weekends with my girlfriends, romantic escapes with my husband, artist dates, family vacations and women's retreats that I organize each year as a part of my business. Getaways fuel joy through experience. When you remove yourself from the familiar, you experience you outside of your normal limits. I treasure these getaways often much more than my physical possessions.

I know for a fact that getaways with my husband have kept our marriage alive, have kept our communication flowing and have created a very stable and happy family. Some people could accuse me of neglecting or walking away from my children when we made those getaways a priority when the children were toddlers. Now that my kids are adults, I look back and know that we did the right thing. Our children knew that their parents were happy and in love. We remained connected as a team so that we could really create a stable, safe and loving family environment at home. I recommend that anyone with children, especially small children, make getaways with their spouse a regular priority.

When you enter into the retreat experience of any kind, no matter what kind of getaway you're choosing, you move away from the familiar physical world as you step closer to your true essence. On retreat you can let go of the daily routines and take on new ways. You may eat differently, sleep in unfamiliar beds, yet you remain the same person. Retreats allow you to know more about who you really are when your world gets shaken up and changed a little bit.

Several times each year I take an escape to my family's cottage in the historic town of Lakeside, Ohio on Lake Erie. It is an easy 75-minute drive from my home, yet a clear break with my routine and always a magical place. Sometimes my Lakeside getaways become mostly about cleaning and yard work, because there is plenty of work to be done with a summer cottage that isn't always in use. There are also times when I go there with my husband and extended family during the summer to enjoy swimming, concerts and cultural events in this wonderful community. I often find myself planning weekends at the cottage so that a small group of my closest friends can share long walks, shopping, cooking, great wine and deep conversation.

In 2006 I started holding an annual woman's retreat in Lakeside each spring. I chose Lakeside because it is a place of clear energy, strong spiritual heritage and natural beauty. It is a comfortable home away from home. It nurtures the soul and is the kind of place you want to leave home for. It's also the kind of place that stays in your heart long after you leave. With the beautiful coast of Lake Erie and the grounding energy of limestone beneath your feet, giant old trees and beautifully restored homes and gardens throughout, it serves as a splendid combination when it comes to a place that fosters balanced energy flow. I'm so grateful to have found it.

I expect miracles each time I come to this magical place, and I watch for these to unfold every time. A magical place like Lakeside allows my guests to easily find their wise, inner voice, really listen to it and become comfortable with the messages it brings. That's why I love bringing people here.

Recommended Escapes

I hope you are beginning to think of the perfect escape for recharging your energy. Just in case you were wondering, I have many suggestions for getaways of all sizes. Here are some of my all-time favorites, including my comments:

Ohio Favorites

The Inn at Honey Run, Millersburg OH
www.innathoneyrun.com 330-674-0011
In the heart of Amish country, this has been a favorite place for my annual girls' getaway to the Garden Symposium held in late January each year. My husband and I have also enjoyed wonderful romantic getaways here. Fall is absolutely heavenly.

Marblehead Peninsula/Lakeside, OH on Lake Erie
www.lakesideohio.com

This historic lakeside community founded in the late 1800s is like stepping back in time. The energy here is incredible and healing. During the summer season (late June to Labor Day) you will pay a fee to enter, which includes admission to abundant educational and arts programming. One of my favorite girlfriend getaways is the Tour of Homes and Craft Show, held in late July each year. Idlewyld B&B is a great place to stay and also home base for The Indigo Connection's annual women's retreat in mid-May. Lakeside is just a short walk or bike ride from the dock where you can hop on the ferry to Kelley's island www.kelleysisland.com where you can enjoy a day or exploring, biking, hiking, camping or dining near the water.

Geneva on the Lake/Ohio Wine Region
www.visitgenevaonthelake.com

The wineries in this area are outstanding and reminded me of many we visited in Napa and Sonoma. My favorite place to stay is **The Lake House Inn & Winery** www.thelakehouseinn.com. They have a variety of beautiful rooms, suites and cabins, a home-cooked breakfast, a great restaurant and winery, and a patio overlooking the water. This is the place for beautiful sunsets. Also recommended is **The Eaglecliff Inn** www.eaglecliffinn.com. Although not on the water, it has a great front porch for people-watching and a delicious hot breakfast each morning.

Other Recommended Destinations for Escape

Maui Passage www.thepeacefulwoman.com

The Maui Passage is a week of deep spiritual growth as you bond with a small group of women to explore the land, water, nature, people, culture and history of this beautiful and magical island. You will be transformed through joy, laughter, friendship and experience. Browse itinerary details and videos at www.thepeacefulwoman.com. For information on business partnerships, facilitator opportunities and special discounts contact betsy@theindigoconnection.com

The Outer Banks of North Carolina www.outerbanks.org

If you need to rest, enjoy the beach and love unstructured time to read, sleep, reflect and play, this is an ideal spot for couples, family reunions or groups of several families. Well-appointed rental homes of all sizes are available to meet just about every budget.

Lily Dale Assembly, Lily Dale NY
www.Lilydaleassembly.com

If you want to develop intuition and deepen your belief in the invisible, this is the place to go. Come with an open mind to discover Lily Dale, the world's largest center for spiritual development and the practice of the Spiritualist religion. Spiritualists believe that our bodies may die, but our spirits live on. Since 1879, Lily Dale has offered a world-renowned summer program of lectures, workshops and other activities featuring best-selling authors, leaders in academic and scientific research into psychic phenomena, as well as the world's most powerful mediums, teachers and healers. Lily Dale is a beautiful community filled with historic cottages and lovely gardens, surrounded by a towering old-growth forest. Your $10 gate pass provides access to messages from the resident mediums at Inspiration Stump, lectures and healing services. Private readings, classes and special events may have additional charges.

Port D'hiver Bed & Breakfast in Melbourne Beach, FL
www.portdhiver.com

If you crave an escape from winter and a quick, romantic and affordable weekend on the Florida coast, you've got to check out Port D'Hiver. Just a short hour drive from Orlando International Airport, this charming B&B offers luxurious rooms, daily hot breakfast made to order, a beautiful beach, daily social hour with wine, beer and hors d'oeuvres and great restaurants within walking distance. The friendly atmosphere and attention to detail have made this a favorite long weekend destination when we need a sun escape without the hassle. Book early—this place fills quickly because it is so wonderful.

Sedona, AZ www.visitsedona.com
Red rocks, clear skies and clear energy. You will find vistas, art, history and activities to enlighten your spirit and connect you to the land. Many believe this is a place of great healing energy.

The Pillars Hotel/Fort Lauderdale, FL www.pillarshotel.com
If you need a great place to stay before embarking on a cruise from Fort Lauderdale, or simply need a long weekend at a cozy beach paradise, this is for you. Nestled amidst a tropical garden, just a short walk from the beach on the Intracoastal Waterway, this casual, yet

elegant hotel is well known for its service, gourmet dining and out-standing décor. Just a short 10 minute drive from the Fort Lauder-dale airport makes this a very easy vacation for snowbirds in need of a long weekend to indulge in escape.

Rick Steves European Vacations www.ricksteves.com

Rick knows how to design an amazing European vacation, whether you follow his guide books or enroll in one of the dozens of group tour itineraries. We loved our two-week Southern Italy tour in 2004 because all the details and activity fees were covered, our guides were outstanding people, and we were able to see and do so much more than we would have if we had ventured out on our own. You must be physically fit and able to carry your own bags up steps without whining. This rule works to your advantage when everyone in your tour group moves quickly and joyfully through the sites you really do get more from each vacation day.

Action Time

1. List 10 escapes you hope to experience or accomplish within the next year. Keep in mind that you can choose to escape in some way every single day. List 365 escapes if you like, because you really could do it every day.

2. Choose an item from your list in number one and set a timer for five minutes of daydreaming time that includes the following: Create that place, that time and the surroundings. Add people that you choose to be part of this dream experience, or maybe you want to keep it as a solitary daydream. That's okay, too. Add other sensory perceptions: what do you see, feel, touch, smell and taste as this experience takes place?

   Put yourself in the middle of it and feel appreciation for the beautiful experience you have created and are allowing yourself to enjoy. Pretend that it is happening now and allow your body to show you how that feels. Look deeply within and feel it emotionally, physically and spiritually.

   At the end of five minutes, record the vivid details of your thoughts, emotions, memories and sensations in your journal. Let your imagination continue to roll as you recollect this daydream as if it really, truly happened. Make sure to check in to see how your body feels. Is there any discomfort or hesitation as you flesh out the experience? These hesitations provide clues to negative beliefs that may be blocking you in real life.

3. Are you feeling guilty or undeserving of a magical escape? Is there a reason you don't let yourself do these things? Treat the negative thoughts, blocks or discomfort that may have come up using EFT or another healing method. Accept that you have resistances. Everybody does. Decide if you're going to choose to let them go. Give yourself a break and accept yourself now, just as you are with these human blocks.

4. Create a sacred space to serve yourself and others. Create an affirmation statement to summarize your intentions for the sacred space you will create. Refer to the statement on page 128 for an example.

5. Consider all of the options for retreats or getaways available to you. What kind of getaway will give you the greatest value for your time and investment? What elements of this chapter are you most aware of as you consider your own priorities for escape? Jot down ideas in your journal.

Chapter 8

Awaken the Creator

*"A rock pile ceases to be a rock pile the moment a single man contemplates it,
bearing within him the image of a cathedral."*
Antoine de Saint-Exupery

"I saw the angel in the marble and carved until I set him free."
Michelangelo

My own journey into creativity has been a lifelong one. I was fortunate to be raised by parents who taught me at an early age the value of the arts, to appreciate the many forms creativity takes and to explore my own creative talents. As creative mentors, my parents nurtured me through a wealth of examples in their own lives. My dad was a successful business leader and financial portfolio manager, who prided himself in showing me how creativity was used in sales presentations, speeches and meeting client needs.

My mother, an elementary school teacher, gave me the hands-on creative experiences with paints, crayons, scissors and glue. She allowed me help her cook when I was only two years old, and she was passionate about nature, the garden, exploring the woods and learning about native plants and herbs.

My life as a student also exposed me to creative aspects of music and performance. I participated in choir and studied piano and flute over the course of my school days. I especially excelled with the flute and enjoyed a first chair position in band and orchestra throughout high school.

As an adult I have merged creativity into all areas of my life, as a business owner, marketer, speaker, writer, parent, homeowner, gardener, cook, wife and community volunteer. It has been rewarding in more ways than I can count.

I initially assumed that everyone was creative, but later came to realize that most people have not been nurtured with the positive experiences that I have enjoyed. I was one of the lucky ones. In spite of all of the positive reinforcement and creative success, I continually discover that I, too, carry creative blocks. I have fears within me about being creative and sharing my creations with the bigger world.

What Kind of Creator Are You?

We are all creators. When we create we become fully alive. We are all part of an endless, enormous act of creation. We are a creative miracle unfolding.

Something occurred to me long ago: when we create we are fully alive. Maybe I'm most aware of this because I create constantly in so many areas of my life. I create in my mind and in the physical dimension, too.

My mother has often remarked about my innate ability to create things out of tiny scraps of fabric, old furnishings or an assortment of random materials that come into my possession. I am admittedly an extreme creator who easily manifests an idea into physical form. It's funny that it took decades of other people's reflections to help me realize that I have a gift for creativity and it is extraordinary. I get excited about creativity, and that's why there's a whole chapter dedicated to it in this book.

This chapter is my effort to help pass along my love for the creative spark, and also to help you become a stronger creative force in your own realm of influence. As a business owner, creation is an incredible cycle that begins with a thought, then grows and blossoms into a fully manifested message, product or service. To witness creation is to be part of a miracle.

The notion of creativity also gets me thinking about those opposing low times in life. I've often wondered if depression is the absence of that spark of creation. Through creation, can depression be healed? I am hopeful that the answer is "yes." I've seen people light up after spells of depression and it seems that as they light up they return to a very creative process of some sort.

To be of service, we can all encourage each other to be creative beings. There are more ways to create than can easily be listed here. Songs, words, textiles, cooking, decorating, jewelry, hairstyles, speeches, musical performance, gardening, floral design, marketing, new product development and relationships are all creative possibilities. You can choose creation as a means to be successful and fully alive.

The Good News

The good news is that creativity can be easily awakened through a process of self-awareness and self-discovery. Each of us is here for a reason, and when we give ourselves permission to create without fear, we do truly come alive. As we let ourselves be creative, we also fulfill our purpose and offer valuable service to the world around us. This cycle of fulfillment and service is what brings joy and transforms our world into a better place.

Overcoming Our Blocks

Is perfection practical? Even the most creative people find themselves blocked, reluctant and uncertain at times. There is no such thing as perfect, yet we struggle and we reach for it. We waste energy worrying about being judged, not being good enough, forgetting something or not having the capacity to do what is being asked of us. True creativity requires that we stretch beyond our current position yet accept that there will always be someone out there who might do it better than we did. Is it worth trying anyway? You bet!

Imagine if the author of your favorite book or story kept those words to herself because she was afraid it wasn't perfect. Imagine life if all those performers you love so dearly chose to hide behind the curtain instead of becoming the artists that they are today. Every creator has to expose his or her work to critics to gain the confidence that comes through the experience of trial and error. Are you denying your fans the gift of your ideas, art, inspiration, music or wisdom?

I, too, suffered from creative blocks. I've been working on this book since 2005, but throughout the creative process, my fears and doubts got in the way. I would continue to put the manuscript aside. I'd criticize it and stop writing. I finally could no longer tolerate the delay. I've decided to release this book, even though it will never be perfect. My primary hope is that your life is enriched in some way by the ideas shared on these pages.

Don't allow fear to hold you back. Acknowledge your fear. Admit it and accept it for what it is. Once that acceptance is behind you, go out and create something anyway. Use EFT tapping or heart massage treatment to rebalance and move your energy. Deliberately choose how you would rather be and feel. Speak kind words to the timid creator inside of you. Treat that scared part of yourself as you would a frightened child. Befriend it and turn on the light so your soul can see how to create from a place of love.

Becoming Energetically Relevant

One of our greatest fears as creators is that we might be ignored. We'll make something and nobody will want to buy it, pay for it or give it any attention. It certainly stings to be invisible and possibly poor, too, after all that hard work. The term "starving artist" is a common way of referring to exactly that situation.

How can an artist get attention and attract more clients, money and success? The answer is energetic relevance. Think of the situation like this. Creation requires combining what the world around you needs with the solution that solves that need in a unique and effective way. A creative solution relates and has value. When creativity is combined with relevance, the artist is well paid.

Facebook's founder Mark Zuckerberg is a great example of this. When he created Facebook, he created a solution for a need we didn't even know we needed. For that, he has been paid handsomely, and rightly so. Serve your audience as you create and everyone will win.

Expressing Our Creative Nature: Merging The Artist's Way with EFT

As we approach releasing our full creative potential, each of us must consider how our personal energy flow could be enhanced or if creative blocks are inhibiting our process.

I had frequently heard people mention the book *The Artist's Way* by Julia Cameron as a must read. I finally got around to reading the book in 2005, one chapter per week over the course of 12 weeks. I dutifully completed the chapter exercises, three daily "morning pages" in my journal, and took myself on weekly artist dates, just as the book suggested. I confronted my fears about failure, success and judgment. What was unique about my venture into *The Artist's Way* was that I had this incredible tool, EFT, to help me process the negative thoughts and emotions that inevitably surfaced while making my way through the book.

Subsequently I found my business thriving, doors opening and opportunities emerging for me. I had discovered the perfect pairing between creativity and emotional freedom in my life. I soon realized that I needed to share what I had discovered for the benefit of others. In 2006 I gathered my first "Artist's Way with EFT" study group at a local wellness center, with the intention of sharing the book, offering group support and demonstrating applications of EFT with the material in each chapter.

I watched my groups discover things about themselves that had been stuffed away for years. I witnessed their tears, forgiveness, shame, regret and anger. I watched them build confidence, better relationships, self-worth and intestinal fortitude to stand up for their own truth.

I was particularly touched by their miracles and synchronicities as they blossomed as creative souls in uncountable ways. The use of EFT brought immediate relief for uncomfortable emotions and the unpleasant memories that the book stirs up. I realized that I was onto something amazing.

Groups and the Creation of EFT Treatment Statements

Over the next three years I facilitated six more "Artist's Way with EFT" groups. I eventually added teleclasses and found that these worked just as well as the live meetings. It was through the teleclasses that I began recording the EFT treatment sequences and awakened to awareness of how divine universal flow was working in a powerful way through me. As I transcribed these recordings I, too, was inspired by the statements. I now had something more I could share with the world.

In Appendix III, you'll some of my favorite EFT scripts for clearing resistance and creative blocks. These are actual statements transcribed from live teleclass sessions, inspired by *The Artist's Way*, combined with the specific needs of the people who gathered with me to explore their creative nature. You will notice that the statements contain many powerful affirmations to propel creators into joyful productivity. I'm grateful to Julia Cameron and every client and student who has helped me to gain a better understanding of the creative process. The journey of creative discovery never ends.

Enhanced Flow through Chakra Awareness

As I continued teaching EFT with *The Artist's Way*, I soon discovered that yet another piece of the puzzle was missing. That missing piece was the awareness of chakras. Ancient traditions honor chakras as powerful spinning energy centers or vortices in the body. Each of the seven chakras has a connection to specific human characteristics and also organ systems. My experience has shown me time and again how chakras are highly relevant to the study of creativity.

Consider the seven chakras as a rainbow of possibilities, giving clues to your strengths as well as your weaknesses. Because the chakras have a connection to specific parts of the body, often we notice that there are physical symptoms connected with areas of blocked energy flow. I encourage you to pay attention to your own body as I briefly review the chakras below. As you read this, consider whether you might have strength in that chakra or a potential block that needs attention.

1. **Root or Base**
   The root chakra represents basic human needs, such as food, water, shelter, survival, safety and of course money. Located at the base of the spine, the color for this chakra is red. The root chakra is your connection to the earth. You are uniquely created to dwell on earth and to be connected to the earth. But if you don't feel safe, that's difficult to do. By connecting and unblocking this

chakra and being fully connected to the earth, you can draw energy from the earth to sustain your system. Pay attention to your basic feelings about safety and if you have issues with money, this is a good chakra to pay particular attention to as well.

2. Sacral

This chakra is represented by the color orange and located below the navel in the lower abdominal and pelvic area. The sacral chakra is associated with the sexual organs, lower back, hips and lower digestive tract. Oftentimes the blocks around this chakra involve sexual identity and creative expression. Blocks can arise here due to sexual abuse, infertility, childbirth, suppressed sexual desires and any negative beliefs you may be holding about your sexuality.

3. Solar Plexus

This chakra is represented by the color yellow and can be located two inches above the navel. This chakra is connected to the stomach, pancreas, liver and the skin. This energy center has a lot to do with your work, vocation and how you exercise your power in the world. It is very much a part of your creative nature and the way you express yourself as a valuable part of society.

4. Heart

The heart chakra is represented by the color green. This chakra is in the middle of the seven chakras. It is energetically where the energies of heaven and earth meet within you. As you close your eyes and focus your attention on the heart, you effectively center your energy. The heart chakra encompasses not only the heart but also the lungs, shoulders, upper back and breasts. The heart chakra is related to giving and receiving love as well as the expression of forgiveness and compassion. Blocks in the heart chakra can arise through grief, rejection, heartbreak and especially romantic break-ups.

5. Throat

Throat is represented by the color blue and includes the thyroid glands, mouth, teeth, jaw and neck. This chakra is highly connected to expression, voice, and communication. Blocks in throat energy can reveal themselves through inflexibility, indecisiveness, repressed emotions or repressed opinions.

6. **Third Eye**

This chakra is represented by the color indigo, a dark purple-blue. It is located between the eyebrows and is represented by the pineal gland. The third eye center also includes the eyes, ears, nose and forehead. Intuition and higher consciousness are related to this chakra. If this chakra is blocked you may experience headaches, sinus problems or trouble with your hearing or vision. Pay attention to this chakra, especially if you desire to open more of your intuitive capacity.

7. **Crown**

This energy center is represented by the color lavender and is located at the top or crown of the head. The crown is associated with your connection to the divine and unlimited energy from Source/God that flows through each of us. The crown chakra encompasses going with the flow, faith, higher consciousness, and balanced awareness. Consider this chakra very important because it gives you access to unlimited energy. Setting the intention that your crown is open and connected to Divine Source will assure you an abundant, balanced and flowing energy supply.

Moving Meditation

One of the best ways to unblock a stifled creator is to get them moving. Here's a great quote:

> *"I have never had so many good ideas day after day*
> *as when I worked in a garden."*
> John Erskine.

You may have been told that you must sit still and meditate regularly to be able to get your greatest creative downloads. As much as I know meditation is a good thing and has brought me some phenomenal results, I personally have a hard time sitting still for long periods of time. When you have a long list of things to do it can be even harder to sit still and create. That's where moving meditation can be your salvation.

Have you ever noticed that when you engage in a mundane task like washing dishes, pulling weeds or taking a walk, your creative ideas begin to flow? Why is that? There is something in mundane action that gets you into your body, keeps your left logical brain busy, but somehow frees up that creative right side of the brain to engage in extra fun. This is mindful multi-tasking at its very best.

When I find myself stuck or simply in need of new creative angles on a project or situation, I often choose running as the way I both escape and also connect with the wise voice that lives inside of me. Running helps me breathe deeply, connect with nature, get my feet on the ground and work off stress. I also know it's doing more than that. I am creating ideas, testing flow for an upcoming presentation or crafting the perfect wrap-up exercise for a retreat as I breathe, sweat and push my body down the road. I return from a run feeling inspired and often need to find paper to catch it all before I get distracted.

The garden is another place I often turn to for moving meditation. Dead-heading flowers, weeding, harvesting and arranging things from my garden is a boost for creative flow that I often choose. It feels good to be doing something productive while also lost in thought and mesmerized by the beauty of nature. What kinds of moving meditations work this kind of magic for you? I urge you to experiment and see what you discover about your own creative flow as you try some of these:

- Cleaning a bathroom
- Folding laundry
- Walking at sunset
- Baking
- Vacuuming
- Watering plants
- Dusting
- Washing the car
- Riding a bike
- Reading
- Trimming hedges
- Spreading mulch
- Mending clothes
- Walking in the early morning
- Polishing silver
- Mowing the lawn
- Walking the dog
- Pushing a stroller

You can probably think of more, but this gives you an idea. Productive actions that need to be done can engage your mind while you move, so that you can also create.

Vision Boards Amplify the Energy of Creation

Creation is a process of seeing possibilities for the future and getting clear about your desires. I personally dedicate a good portion of the week between Christmas and New Year's every year to immerse myself in a process that results in completion of a new a visual representation of my hopes and dreams and all that I hold dear—my vision board.

Before jumping into creation of a vision board I recommend taking time to take stock of the year that just ended. If you already have a vision board, pull it out. Take a look at it. How did you do? If you have a journal you can take a look at your original list of goals and resolutions. You can also review your calendar from the year that just ended to recollect the highlights, accomplishments and the struggles that you've encountered each month. Ask yourself, "What was the theme of this year that just passed? What did I learn? What am I still trying to do or discover?"

As you reflect on your notes and accomplishments, see what played out well and where you remain blocked. Were there some desires that still escaped you? Did your objectives shift during the year to new priorities that were not represented on the vision board? That's okay, too.

Take note of what you are most grateful for from the year ending. List these items as part of your personal farewell to the year. If there are items on this list that you continue to hold dear for the future, make sure to include them in some way on the vision board that you're creating now. There is no right or wrong way to do a vision board. If your completed board stirs up joyful, positive emotions, you have definitely succeeded.

This may be the first time you've done a vision board so I offer the following thoughts and suggestions to help get you get started:

Size

Vision boards can be any size: 8 ½ x 11 inch standard paper works just fine and frames well. I've also seen people create wonderful portable vision boards on manila file folders. Feel free to create a massive board on huge poster size paper. Size is optional and so is the shape. Start small and grow. You can choose to create multiple boards to represent different areas of your life. If you have more than one office or work location, you might choose to place an uplifting vision board at all locations.

Images

Choose images that really pull at your heart. These can be animals, scenes, colors, water, sky, people, adventures, logos, places you hope to see, things you hope to own, representations of something you hope for and symbols that you love. Include words or phrases that carry strong meaning for you. Inspirational quotes or poems are also great additions to your vision board. Create and print words and phrases from your computer if you can't find them in magazines.

Materials

Consider integrating fabrics, textures, dried plant materials, beads or stones into your design. You can use markers, paints and pastels, too. You might also want to dab on your favorite essential oil to enhance the sensory experience.

Photos and People

Remember to include an image of yourself somewhere. Throw in a few photos of people you love to be with. Dare to put your own photo with somebody special you hope to meet, someone famous or the soul mate that is missing from your life picture. Perhaps you'll want to put your head on a different body. That's okay, too. You are permitted to take bold, creative expression here and have a little fun.

Two-Sided Boards

If you run out of room for all the images, do what I do and complete both sides of the vision board, even if only one side faces you most of the time. This reinforces the energy of the board and is perfectly fine. If you checked out my personal boards from the past two years, you'd find my previous board hidden behind the frame. You might even want to make a hanging mobile version of your vision board if you have limited wall space. Even if images can't be seen, the energy is there to support you.

Displaying Your Board

Once your board is complete, place it in a spot where it'll be seen regularly. I know many people who prefer to put it on their bathroom mirror. I like to position my board near my telephone and computer so that I can gaze at it often while working. Share your boards with a few trusted friends and help support each other's goals in the year ahead. I look forward to supporting the seekers and self-care enthusiasts now and well into the future. Please keep in touch with me and let me know how you are using your vision boards to create and manifest your dreams.

Share Creation and Enjoy the Ride

Don't just create things. Share them, too. You cannot grow without the experience of exposure. I know it feels naked to put yourself out there and share what you've just created, especially when you are unsure if you're any good yet. I often feel that way, too, but have learned to do it anyway.

One of the exercises in Julia Cameron's book The Artist's Way asks participants to create an Artist Prayer. You too may want to create a prayer for the creator who lives within you.

Betsy's Artist Prayer

I celebrate the dawn of each new day as I count my many blessings
My divine creator is near, whispering softly to my heart.
As I demonstrate my love for myself, I send love to all.
Following the subtle nudges, my heart opens to exquisite peace.
Keep me supported and safe within this powerful connection.
Allow me to fulfill my destiny as I follow your Divine will.

Practice Time

1. Take a moment to reflect upon the beliefs and fears that keep you from creating and sharing your creations fully with others. What are you really good at creating? What situations have caused you to hold back or worry about perfection? Use one of the EFT tapping scripts for creativity in Appendix III to address this block. What do you notice?

2. Collect pictures, words and images that inspire you and represent your dreams. Create a vision board and dare to share it with a special friend. Schedule a time to create these boards together if you'd like, and plan to verbalize your dreams as you share your vision boards together. Don't forget to place your board in a prominent place so you can admire it regularly.

3. Review the seven chakras and answer the following questions as they apply to your experience:

    a. Which energy center is your strongest? Why?

    b. Which of your chakras is most blocked? How do you know? How does this block protect or serve you? What benefits do you receive by having this block?

    c. Close your eyes and place both hands on the area of your body with the blocked energy. As you breathe in, imagine the color and the spin of this chakra building. As you exhale, allow the block to relax. Imagine what you would create if you no longer carried any blocks in this center. See what comes to mind and jot it down.

4. Identify individuals or groups that could be part of an ongoing support system for you as an artist and creator. Reach out and engage deeper connection with these people. Dare to share your creative efforts with a supportive audience.

Chapter 9

Faith in the Invisible

"There are two ways to live: you can live as if nothing is a miracle; you can live as if everything is a miracle."
Albert Einstein

"It is only with the heart that one can see rightly; what is essential is invisible to the eye."
Antoine de Saint-Exupery

The Gift of Awareness

As the awareness of energy flow takes place within the framework of your life, you'll soon realize that you are interacting with the invisible world more and more. When I first began to interact with energy by doing the five Tibetan exercises, I was simply curious and hopeful about retaining my youth. As energy started balancing and moving within my body, it was as though a door to this invisible power opened. Although I had always been a spiritual person and attended church regularly, I was suddenly finding myself more deeply spiritual than ever before.

I came to eventually understand that energy is spirit and that energy of spirit doesn't necessarily need a body to be present and interacting with us. Being more energy aware will also bring you a new appreciation of how the physical world and daily life is a huge part of your energy experience. You will begin to pick up on emotional shifts more quickly, notice small changes in your physical health and gain a new appreciation for how you can work with the present moment to create better outcomes.

This opening of ongoing present moment awareness keeps you firmly planted in the now both physically and energetically. As you live in the state of presence you will also notice more synchronicity, strokes of good fortune and resources that appear exactly when you need them, almost by magic. Your new awareness will help you realize, just as the Einstein quote at the beginning of this chapter stated, that miracles need not be massive to count. Everything is a miracle. All of the miraculous visible and invisible energy that is part of all creation will help you live with a greater sense of peace.

Faith in the invisible has allowed me to stop worrying about illness, loss, danger and death. Instead, I can more fully focus on living. I trust that you will become more aware of evidence of a higher power in your life as well. Each day will bring new opportunities for you to trust, hope and love—the essential and invisible ingredients that create miracles.

The gift of awareness and the ability to have faith in the invisible has certainly enriched my life. It has given me the ability to see beauty in very small moments and an appreciation for the fact that my thoughts are the energy creating my experience. Even if they're small, unintentional thoughts they are creating a signal.

The Story of the Big Rock and a Wish

Last summer I was enjoying some relaxation time up at Lake Erie at my parent's cottage. It was a luxurious time when my dog, Gracie, and I had the house to ourselves.

One evening Gracie and I decided to take a sunset walk along the lakefront path. We soon approached a big flat rock along the shore that I visit often. I love this rock as a place to sit and meditate. It was a little different this time because I had Gracie, my 100-pound golden retriever with me. Gracie hates to be separated from me, and I knew that if I climbed up on that rock, Gracie would be upset because she would be left behind on the ground. This rock was more than three feet tall and it was unlikely that Gracie could make that sort of a jump.

I decided to climb up on the rock anyway, hoping Gracie could just hang out on the ground patiently while I meditated. It didn't quite go that way. Gracie was immediately upset that she was still on the ground while I was on the rock. I began to think that I would much prefer to have us both up there too.

That small thought must have taken root because suddenly Gracie took a big leap and there she was, right next to me. I thought to myself, "This is a miracle. That's a huge leap for a 100-pound dog." In my mind I thought to myself immediately, "Wouldn't it be nice if someone would come along and take our picture because nobody's going to believe this." Next thing you know, within 60 seconds, a nice man and his little daughter approached and asked if they could take our picture! He had a camera and he was more than happy to also take a picture with the camera that was miraculously still in the pocket of my pants.

Figure 3 - Betsy and Gracie on the big rock

The photo is here in the book for you to enjoy as evidence that it really happened. It was a small moment in terms of the bigger scheme of my life and the life of the planet, but it was a delicious moment nonetheless. It is something I'll always remember. You may be skeptical about creating reality from your thoughts, but I'm going to own that memory as a miracle. As you begin to see more things as miracles you'll create more delicious experiences for yourself too.

Surrender to the Invisible

There will be times when it seems as though you are alone, cut off and isolated from the Divine Source. When you find yourself alone without an answer, it can be hard to have faith. *The Surrender Prayer* mentioned in Chapter 3 is your answer for times like these. You've got to surrender to the bigger plan and wait patiently. Surrender is the most comfortable way to survive and speed up that waiting time. Instead of fighting what is, your energy is more available to attract what is manifesting for you. I've had many times when I've used this kind of prayer in those moments when I wonder where God went.

There aren't too many of those lost moments for me anymore. Through surrender and asking for help, you'll find God will show up in the form of a messenger, a resource or something to help ease your pain or to increase your understanding of the "why." Don't forget to ask friends, family or others for help, too. Eventually we must emerge from a place of fear and isolation to reconnect with the world around us. Tapping to the *Surrender Prayer* as an energetic act of surrender will help you feel more like taking the next appropriate action. Trust me on this and try it for yourself. You can view a video demonstration of the *Surrender Prayer* at www.energymakeover4U.com.

Divine Guidance

What about all those important decisions that you must make in daily life? Is there a way to connect to infinite intelligence to arrive at the best answer? The answer is "yes" and it comes from sending that specific question deliberately out to a higher power for the answer. I must caution you that higher power has far more answers and possibilities than you could ever imagine. The answers that you get back may be strange and confusing.

Often you'll get a metaphor or a puzzle to solve. God has this funny sense of humor when it comes to giving the guidance we request. God asks us to stretch our muscles and make sense of it. By stretching our muscles we do indeed become stronger, and that's really what our Divine creator wants of us, that stronger version of ourselves.

Asking and Receiving

Just about everyone has heard the statement, "It is more blessed to give than to receive," in some form or fashion. We drill it into our kids' heads at Christmas and we accept it as truth ourselves, too. As a person in the healing and service profession I find myself constantly in the giving mode, which I've chosen and which is very satisfying. To be able to give and be prosperous enough to give is a blessing.

I remember a time several years ago when I decided to participate in the monthly open healing night at the wellness center where I worked. It was the first time that I'd ever done this. Not knowing how it worked, I assumed that I was going to be donating and giving my healing energy to others throughout the evening. What I learned once I got there was that we would all take turns healing each other and that I, too, would receive healing.

Suddenly I found myself in a new, vulnerable place, yet a place I certainly needed to be. How arrogant I had been to think that healing goes only one way. In fact, how could I possibly be an effective healer unless I received, too? It is the nature of balance. But it was not a notion that completely reached my awareness.

Receiving is not about keeping score. I now look at receiving as a metaphor for the sacred feminine, a part of the natural life cycle. By resisting the process of receiving or accepting gifts from others, we are also likely to lose energy in the process as we deny the energy of the giver and all the blessings or gifts they offer. Only by receiving do we complete the healthy circuit and restore the energetic harmony that the universe loves.

If you're always in the giving mode, ask yourself how you might switch places for once. Mothers can become embedded in the giving mode, taking care of families, husbands and even the people at work. Look for ways you could acknowledge the gifts of others by asking them to help and support you. Allow people to return favors or nurture you while letting you feel that you truly deserve their care and attention. Count your blessings and be grateful for what you receive. The greatest blessings occur in the presence of balanced giving and receiving.

Trust Amidst Chaos

Trust is a topic worthy of consideration. Trust is invisible, if I need to remind you of that. In your business, you want your clients and customers to trust you. As a customer you want to trust the people you have chosen to do business with. Trust defines and binds individuals together in extremely positive ways. When you can fully trust others you are safe, secure and fairly treated, and that feels great.

Trust is a skill that also applies to the law of attraction. You attract what you are, what you think and what you believe. We ask for more and wait patiently for the universe to respond. Does getting what you ask for make you feel more trusting and safer? In many ways it does. Getting what you ask for allows you to know that something is responding. Noticing when you get what you requested can be the greater challenge.

Successful attraction requires living in the present, something that we know is good but yet have trouble doing. It's often said, "Be careful what you wish for." Nothing could be truer, yet it goes way beyond this. Just wishing isn't enough. Your emotions must be positive and uplifting in order for the best outcomes to take shape. Doubts and deception are energies that can get in the way.

What if the universe doesn't provide the response you had hoped for, or perhaps gives no response at all? Does that mean you sent the wrong signal? Were your signals mixed up? Did you miss the responses that were sent your way because you weren't paying attention? Feeling trust becomes difficult if we become impatient. Worries start to dominate our thinking as we allow doubt to creep in. Doubt sends a signal, too, which shuts down the attraction process, which we thought we had deliberately put into motion.

It is said that there are really only two emotions: love and fear. Trust is just another form of love. Doubt is a lonely feeling that is a variation of fear. If you desire to be more trusting, you have to act in a way that attracts trust. Think in terms of trusting unconditionally and behave as though the universe is responding to your trusting requests.

Believe it is so. Feel the joyful vibration of receiving what you have asked for, rather than the fear of being without it. Catch yourself in the moment of doubtful thinking and transform those doubts to hopeful information. Speak your hopes, feel them and experience them in the present moment of your thoughts.

Below are affirmation statements to allow emotions of security, love and trust to come through for you:

- The universe responds to my requests.

- I safely express my needs from a place of joy.

- The health of my body responds to my thoughts and words in positive ways.

- I am the creator of my experience. I choose to create what is best for all involved.

- I notice the subtle, good things that are happening around me in each moment."

- My positive thoughts bring the perfect people, resources and ideas to my life.

- My life is full of beauty, for which I am grateful.

- I share my good fortune with others, and radiate it through my spirit.

Playing with Space and Time

I was coaching a young mother recently who was having a rough time trying to do it all—mother, wife, artist, fitness enthusiast and a worker, too. Life suddenly didn't seem to be offering her enough time to get all that she needed and wanted into her day. Instead of being excited about the future, she found herself being afraid, burning out and worried that her relationships were suffering. Guilt, frustration and fear were the dominant emotions that she was experiencing.

I've certainly been in her shoes before. I remember that overwhelmed feeling as a new mom working full-time. I spent many of those years in a state of auto pilot. I don't think I was fully present very much of that time. I wish I had known about the self-care tools I now have in my arsenal. I shared with this client a little trick I'd been using which I called "playing with space and time." Whenever I feel overwhelmed or feel as though I've created an impossible situation for myself, I ask God to give me a hand with space and time. I request that a little time warp be created so that all I have to do miraculously fits within this framework. I also ask God to handle the things I am not able to do and the wisdom to know my highest priorities.

When I began playing this game I was very skeptical. I figured that the Law of Attraction was a stretch when it came to time. I first started using the technique for presentations, asking that my material fit exactly into the time available. And you know what happened? It did. Next I started to apply the game to client sessions, especially those where we journeyed into deep meditation and guided regression. When I guided clients into a meditation, the clock kept ticking but we never looked at it. I simply set the intention that time would be handled by God. Soon my clients and I began to emerge from those deep sessions at the perfect time.

Eventually I started applying the space and time game to the long to-do lists on my desk. Delegating time to a higher power really works. I take care of the doing and God handles the passage of time. As I stop worrying about time I can focus on the present. You can do this, too and I have prepared a five minute audio meditation to help you. It's called "Create a Day with Space and Time" and you can listen to it at www.energymakeover4U.com. Give it a try and see if it makes a difference for you.

Something is Out There

Even if you can't see it, something is out there. Think of all the things that enrich your life that you can't see, hear, smell, taste or touch. Yet these things can make a difference. Life is full of surprises and invisible possibilities. Several years ago I took a trip to the spiritualist community of Lily Dale, New York. It was there that I was allowed a deeper awareness of the connection between the physical world and the invisible, spiritual realm that exists in parallel.

We as humans are limited to experiencing a range of frequencies within our physical senses. It is certainly possible that other beings are out there operating in different bandwidths. Something that occurs to me is that expanding human consciousness is exposing us to some new frequencies. Certain places like Lily Dale, New York; Sedona, Arizona; and even my beloved Lakeside, Ohio, may allow frequencies to merge and bandwidths to collide more easily.

The energy vortex theories associated with hundreds of sacred places around the globe seems to make sense, although I doubt anyone has published the official scientific proof. Whether this force is pure energy, God, angels, the souls of lost loved ones or even extra-terrestrial beings could be debated at length.

In Lily Dale I found myself pondering the movie *Contact*, written by the late astronomer and physicist Carl Sagan, and how the lines between physical and non-physical, time and space, life and death may blur in the depths of the unknown. In that movie a brilliant scientist, played by Jodie Foster, was in a state of grief after having lost her father to an illness. As she struggled through her grief, her laboratory research allowed her to suddenly pick up signals from somewhere out in space. Foster's character eventually took part in a space mission to follow the signal. Upon reaching her destination and landing in this faraway place, she was met by her deceased father. The story, although presented as fiction, makes you pause in wonder.

It certainly was a beautiful movie written by a spiritual scientist who, much like Einstein, had studied hard science and come away with faith in the invisible and the depths of what is possible. I believe he would see it the same way I do, that there may just be frequencies and band-widths that are right next to us, but that we have not yet fully merged into our awareness. My personal experience suggests that as humans evolve to perceive a wider range of frequencies, intelligent beings who are able to send and receive energy within that range of perception are drawing near. You might think of this as the fence dividing our two realities becoming lower so that humans can now easily see over the top of it. To me, it means that contact will be increasing. Open your mind to this possibility and do not fear it, for this contact may offer the grace needed to save our planet and the generations to come.

The more we know the less we really know. What is clear is that so many of us are seeking answers to some difficult questions and we are looking for solutions to problems that make our lives difficult. Choosing to have faith in an invisible, wise, intelligent Source in the Cosmos offering free information is certainly an attractive option worth paying attention to. Perhaps this is the same invisible voice that spoke to Einstein, Edison, Sagan and Mother Theresa. That's what I hold in my heart.

In Lily Dale, I experienced an abundance of miracles in a short period of time, both large and small, during three short days. I

Figure 5 - Author Betsy Muller is accompanied by a several orbs
as she speaks at the 2011 ACEP Conference

noticed each situation with a sense of wonder. I come from a science
background, but I no longer need science to convince me that these
phenomena were real because I have developed my own personal
knowing experience.

Some of my experiences in those three days included a session at
the healing temple, the magical beauty of the fairy trail, a personal
message from my grandmother that was channeled to me through a

medium at inspiration stump, a warm presence that surrounded me during an evening ghost walk, and a glorious sunset. Yes, I'll admit that the sunset was visible, but there was more to it than that. It created a deeply spiritual moment, too. Perhaps most intriguing were the mysterious moving lights in the forest which I suspect the skeptics would say were fireflies. I must beg to differ. Those lights were huge and they didn't go on and off as fireflies do. They came closer and they got brighter.

Unexplained Orbs of Light

Orbs are semi-physical balls of light that appear in many of the photos I have taken as well as those taken by many of my friends.

Curiously, the orbs of all sizes are appearing more often in photos when I ask for them (see figure 5). It seems that the more healing work I do and the more I notice the energy intensity of a situation, the more often I'm picking up orbs in the photos that I take. When I share my orb photos with others, they're skeptical, as they should be. I encourage you to be curious about orbs and pay attention to your photos. You can learn more about orbs in the book *Orbs—Their Mission and Messages of Hope*, by former NASA physicist Klaus Heinemann PhD and Gundi Heinemann.

Figure 6 - Two orbs appear against a white wall with George Muller as he thinks of his parents

Dr. Heinemann concludes that orbs are intelligent beings from another dimension and I can't help but agree. I also observe that orbs are attracted to happiness, joy, connection and healing experiences. I once suggested that my husband, George, ask his parents, who are both deceased, to be with him as he sat in front of a bright white wall on a sunny day. I was curious to see if anything would show up in the photo. Sure enough, there was a big orb to the left of his smiling face and a smaller one above the door behind him as shown in figure 6. I could feel in my heart that he brought them there and I could see on the visual screen after that picture was taken that something responded to the call.

It is puzzling that orbs seem to be semi-physical because they show up in front of other images. The visible image of the orb suggests that our frequencies have collided in some way. Orbs are peering over that shorter fence at the edge of our awareness because we've attracted them.

My left brain and science-trained mind want to reject what my heart and experience tells me is true. As I gather these miracles, the more I know, the more I trust my heart. God created all of this and God can never be measured. As hard as science may try, there will always be more yet to be revealed. Einstein kept the following thought on a door in his laboratory at Princeton University which addresses this issue so well:

"Not all that can be counted counts,
and not all that counts can be counted"

I share this in this book because I really believe there is another side. I see it all the time. There is something out there trying to communicate and connect with us, and there is no reason to be afraid. It is the voice that inspires me for my very best creative work. That voice and support is there for you too.

Good things happen when you notice the invisible, act upon it and when you call out for help. Survival of our planet and our species may indeed depend on it. Have faith.

Faith in the Invisible

"Faith is the substance of things hoped for, the evidence of things not seen."
Hebrews 11:1

On Good Friday, we're very much aware in the Christian faith of Jesus' suffering. Good Friday is the day when Jesus' followers lost hope and slipped into grief as they helplessly witnessed his crucifixion. That was a human moment where we all connect to the sadness of loss, the finality of physical death and human grief. Yet we also know that many invisible things took place after the crucifixion to restore faith that was lost. Life triumphed over death later in the story.

The quotation from Hebrews 11:1 was given to me on a plaque by a grateful client several years ago. It hangs in my office today as a constant reminder that my life purpose, mission and business are all about the invisible, unseen forces that enrich and shift our lives.

Reality exists in both physical and non-physical forms, both visible and invisible. We can't necessarily see emotions but they truly exist all around us. Emotions and the energy they carry are strong enough to get our attention and make us pause to check in with the invisible world. Emotions of love, hope, joy and bliss are powerful projectors of energy. Those feelings are radiant, they're hard to miss. The signals of grief, despair, depression and hopelessness form tight and constricted energy fields around the one in pain.

These constricted fields are harder to pick up because low emotion signals are so weak. If anything, we simply feel that pull from a low energy individual that comes when they drain our energy in an effort to replenish their own. We talked about energy vampires in chapter four. You may want to return to that chapter again. Energy drain can happen deliberately or it can happen unintentionally on the part of the weak, depleted person. Either way, it is the suffering person's way of trying to heal the pain that they are carrying.

Many of my friends, subscribers and colleagues know that I've had to say no to lots of things in order to make this book a reality. I admit, there was an invisible force telling me that I must write this book, as much as I don't consider myself an accomplished writer and worry that the world may not even want to read what I write about. I did it anyway. That is what faith inspires within a struggling soul.

I ask you to pay attention and minister to the silent pain that is around you today. Your awareness will guide you to serve in a way that fits who you are. In case you need a little more inspiration I am providing a link to an excellent short video titled "Get Service" at http://tinyurl.com/4ynt38f. I hope you'll watch it and give the message some thought. We can all minister to the pain in the world. Perhaps that's why each of us is here.

Relaxing Into the Perfection of Now

We've covered a lot of invisible, yet energetic forces in this chapter. But perhaps the most important message to leave you with is that you have a choice. You can be worried and obsessed about what's going on in the world or you could relax and begin to trust and have more faith in things that you can't see, touch, feel, smell or hear.

Having faith creates a better reality. Having faith lets you keep your energy intact so that you don't have to leak it in those states of worry and fear. If you spend enough time obsessing you'll find something to be afraid of. But why do that? Why not shift your attention to ways you can be grateful or to all the things that are going right in your life. If worse comes to worst, and things aren't going so great, decide not to waste energy on things you can't change. That really is a mistake because it's never going to make any difference at all. All it does is leave you feeling depleted.

Don't forget about how powerful the act of surrender is. Use the tools and the concepts in this chapter. Just sit back, pause, get your feet flat on the ground, connect to Mother Earth and take that deep breath in. Set the intention that you're rebooting your system, that you can stop the panic and bring a halt to worry. Manipulate space and time to your advantage and get right back into the present moment where you can do something. Now is where you have the power of choice and where you can move on in a state of strength instead of a state of weakness. Energy is that gift. Use the energy you have been given and allow the invisible forces to be part of your team.

Practice Time

1. As much as you have probably released many fears and worries over the years, consider what you may still be holding onto or trying to control without much success. Watch the surrender prayer video at **www.energymakeover4U.com** as you tap your EFT points and think about those things that still worry you. Develop your own surrender prayer based on specific statements to meet your needs. Notice how you feel after tapping to the surrender statements. Jot down your thoughts in a journal. Remember to surrender in times when you don't have answers.

2. Consider the balance of giving and receiving in your own life. List a few examples below of how you are both giving and receiving. As you make your list, ask, "What do I need to ask for or receive more of?" Remember, receiving is just as important as giving.

3. Have you ever noticed orbs or bright spheres of light in your photos? Take a look at a few of your recent photos with a new awareness. Have you found any orbs? As you take photos now, ask for orbs to be present and to be with you. Call in joyful occasions and see what happens. Observe.

4. List three ways you intend to exercise your faith muscles in the year ahead. What will you do even though you are worried or scared? Don't forget to ask for help.

Chapter 10

Mission Accomplished

*"Let yourself be silently drawn by the strange pull of what you really love.
It will not lead you astray."*
Rumi

"Believe those who are seeking the truth. Doubt those who find it."
Andre Gide

*"To find our calling is to find the intersection between our own deep gladness
and the world's deep hunger."*
Frederick Buechner

Your Mission Was Chosen

Each of us is here for a reason and to engage in life in the way that fulfills a sacred mission. You may be thinking to yourself, "What kind of sacred mission could my mundane and rather ordinary life be?" My response to this is: *in spite of what you think; you are most definitely part of the Divine plan and the Divine itself.*

I didn't always believe this. I didn't think there was a big plan and I didn't think I had any choice in the matter. But the longer I live, the more I know that there is a mission. I have learned that if I fail to follow that mission that I chose for myself, there may be disruption in my physical experience. Allow me to explain.

I've talked about many energy experiences throughout this book. I shared how doing the five Tibetan exercises brought about all this awareness, knowing and physical sensation in me. I also wrote about how adding EFT to my life expanded my ability to feel and to be of service to help people. What I haven't shared with you yet is the change in the way my whole spiritual belief system and awareness of my life mission came to be.

You see, I was confused for many years. When my mom gave me the book *Life on the Other Side* by Sylvia Brown in late June 2001, I had never much thought about reincarnation, past lives or spirits without bodies. I had no idea who Sylvia Brown was and hadn't given much thought to the spirit world. Once I read that book, my mind suddenly opened to the possibility of something more. The reason my mind opened was because just one day before that book was handed to me, I had experienced what I can only call a trauma while touring the children's section of the Holocaust museum in Washington, DC with my family.

The experience that I had in the Holocaust Museum was unexplainable. I suddenly found myself in a panic, ran to the restroom and crouched in a stall sobbing for a good 20 minutes. I dried my tears, cleaned up my mascara, emerged from the restroom, rejoined my family (who had been looking for me) and said *nothing* to anybody. I had not talked with a single person about this experience, even as I read that book by Sylvia Brown. The book became real and I began to wonder if I might have reincarnated from a lifetime during the holocaust. I also wondered if a spirit in the museum could have caused my unusual outburst. Many questions surfaced as Sylvia Brown's book comforted me and allowed me to understand that death *is only a transition.*

Interestingly enough, the very next week I found myself at a conference in Switzerland among dozens of people who believed in reincarnation and past life trauma. It was only then that I was curious enough to want to explore past life trauma to see if it existed for me, because I refuse to believe in anything until I have my own experience. The scientist in me says, "If you can't show me the data, give me the experience." Maybe you feel the same way, too.

One of the most memorable events that resulted from attending the Swiss conference in 2001 came during my flight home, when I happened to be seated next to one of the conference workshop leaders, Meryl Beck. Meryl had been practicing EFT and energy psychology for many years. She confidently knew how to help people and I admired her joyful spirit. I hadn't mentioned the trauma in the Holocaust museum, but as we were talking on the plane, something inside me told me I should say something to her about it.

The minute I began sharing the story I suddenly found myself going back into that trauma. I became a sobbing mess on the plane. Fortunately, I was with the right person. Meryl understood that I was carrying a traumatic memory of some sort and she also understood that tapping was the appropriate measure to bring me back, to calm me down and to release whatever it was. My most profound and radical experience with EFT came on that airplane. Meryl had me tap the treatment points while speaking statements that I don't even remember.

What I do remember is that by the time we had finished tapping that last point, I felt a rush of energy come up and out through the top of my head, and leave. From that point on I was never traumatized by the memory of that day in the Holocaust Museum or anything related to that experience. I also came to understand that the emotion I was holding onto as part of that trauma was grief. It was grief so huge that it was impossible for me to fully integrate the feeling.

I don't know whether I lived and was traumatized during the Holocaust, or whether some sort of spirit entity came and took hold of me for a few weeks after my experience in the museum. All I do know is that a simple energy therapy and the help of a gifted practitioner allowed me release that painful disruption permanently, and in just a few short minutes.

Every other energy clearing I've done with EFT tapping since that incident on the plane has always taken place with my feet on the ground. It is typical for me to notice the energy flowing down my legs and into the ground, not up through the crown of my head. Whether this experience had to do with a trauma from another lifetime or a spirit without a body I still do not know and really don't care. Whatever it was that happened, it was over and I came away from it feeling whole, calm and peaceful. It certainly opened up my curiosity about life after death.

From that point on, I've had a series things happen to me that continually remind me that a major part of my soul's mission has to do with sharing what I know.

Life doesn't end at death. Your spirit lives on.

It's all about consciousness. I also believe it is about love. Each step of this journey brings us closer to love. The love that Christ talked about and demonstrated through his life, and the love that almost every single spiritual tradition teaches us is the goal. It is the golden rule. Do to others what you would have them do to you. Living a better life during each lifetime is our mission in the most general sense.

Notice that my lessons about mission came about through some struggles. In 2001, my soul collided with the concept of past life, even though my rational mind didn't want to. I didn't set out wanting to go against my Christian faith or to even give reincarnation the time of day. For the next several years I believed in reincarnation quietly, but dared not share my beliefs in fear that it would alienate my Christian friends.

It wasn't until I was returning from another trip, at another stage of my life that past lives again emerged as an issue I was here to deal with. In this particular instance I'd just finished a major part of my training to become an ACEP certified energy health practitioner (CEHP). This credential was very important to me because I desired formal training, ethical guidelines and the support of colleagues through a professional organization.

By May 2006, I had completed the reading, online exams and three days of live classroom training in California. All that remained was working with a seasoned practitioner with a PhD who would supervise and critique my work for at least 20 hours. It was exciting to know I was near completion.

What happened next was a surprise. I had returned home from San Francisco on a Thursday evening, had a light dinner and went straight to bed. I remember being awakened suddenly in the middle of the night with horrible pains in my abdomen. Pains so serious I could barely breathe. Being the self-care nut that I am, I got out of bed and went downstairs. I drank water and tried tapping my EFT acupoints to relieve the pain. The pain wasn't letting up at all. I became very frightened.

When I went to the bathroom I discovered that I was bleeding internally. I denied it and went back to bed. I struggled through the rest of the night, tossing and turning. When I woke in the morning the bleeding was severe. I took myself to a clinic and from there I was immediately rushed to the hospital. I thought to myself, "How could this be happening? Is this a sign I've made the wrong choice to become certified? I chose this profession. Is God leaving me on my own after I followed what I was told to do?"

There was no explanation. The scans and the tests came back suggesting it might be diverticulitis, but that didn't make sense. I never had digestive problems or intestinal problems before and I eat a healthy diet too. I was released from the hospital without a full explanation directed to follow up in a few months. In the meantime I had to take it easy. And take it easy I did, whether I liked it or not.

After about a month I was given permission to resume normal activities, including my exercises. As a fitness enthusiast, I was ecstatic to return to my normal life. Getting active again was harder than I thought it would be. I was sluggish, slow and noticed pains where I didn't used to have pains before.

I distinctly remember that day in late June 2006 when I was supposed to meet some friends for breakfast but quickly realized I had to cancel. I awakened feeling horrible and my heart was racing. I hooked myself up to my HeartMath computer monitor and discovered my rate was 135 beats per minute. That was a shock. I normally have a 75 beat per minute heart rate. Something was clearly wrong.

I took it easy that day and scheduled a visit with my doctor. Soon I was diagnosed with hyperthyroidism, which meant that my thyroid gland was producing significantly more hormone than normal. The treatment for this kind of ailment includes putting a patient on beta blockers to slow down the heart, while also administering medication that slowly kills the thyroid gland. The cure we were implementing was stabilization, eventually ending with iodine radiation therapy to kill my thyroid gland. As I followed the standard protocol, I wondered "Why is this happening now?" My life has always valued health and balance. I really felt like God was betraying me again.

What I missed at that time was that God had a new lesson for me. As I continued struggling with this new ailment, resources were moving in my direction. The first resource was Dr. Issam Nemeh, MD, an acupuncturist who is also known as a faith healer. I had heard about him through many people and because I wasn't happy with the way the traditional medical community wanted to cure my thyroid, I sought out Dr. Nemeh as an alternative, because I've always responded well to acupuncture.

What I experienced with Dr. Nemeh during my visit was exquisite. It was like being with God for an hour. I definitely had a release of energy and I immediately felt better. I believed I was healed. I walked out of his office feeling lighter and freer than I had almost my entire life. Pure joy would be the best way to describe the feeling that day. I learned through this experience to receive healing and I am certain that I also integrated some new healing frequencies from Dr. Nemeh that have become part of the healing energy I offer to every client.

My endocrinologist was a pessimist and continued monitoring my thyroid gland for the next several months. Of course I had to take it easy. I'd been through a lot. I tapered off of my medications with help from Cheryl Leuthaueser, DO, a gifted holistic physician and friend who believes in miracles. My test results were now normal and I was feeling stronger each day.

As my health returned, I was beginning to feel guilty that I had done nothing to complete my clinical hours for certification. Almost as soon as I had that thought, I received a letter from Barbara Stone, PhD, who had recently moved to Ohio and was offering to serve as my consultant for my certification. I contacted Barbara and agreed to meet with her the very next week.

What I didn't know about Barbara when I first arranged this meeting was that she called herself a *Soul Detective* and specialized in past life regressions. It didn't take long for Barbara to help me realize that my soul was crying for attention. I had some healing to do before I could fully emerge as a healer.

Energy Heals the Soul

Barbara helped me see and have a very powerful awareness of how energy healing heals the soul. What she and I learned in our work together was that I had several past lives where I was a "wounded healer." During those lives I had encountered individuals who took me down. In one of the lives I encountered a resentful former lover who put a curse on me that eventually killed me. In another life I had been ostracized and accused of getting in over my head as a midwife. I was held responsible by a Roman soldier for killing his wife and two unborn twins. I had fallen into a deep depression and died in that life without having resolved my grief and my guilt over that event. You can read about two of my past life cases in Barbara Stone's book, *Invisible Roots*.

Barbara guided me back in time to women who are part of my soul history. In going back, we had conversations with those souls, did healing work, and brought the healing forward to my present life. I was afraid to fully become a healer in this life because I had been wounded severely and my soul remembered that. My health problems were energetic reflections of the distress my soul held about returning to the role of healer. By clearing the energy of the past trauma, both the physical problems and my reluctance as a practitioner melted away.

Today I have become more comfortable talking with clients and friends about past lives and those things that don't quite fit into the Christian tradition. I want to stay connected, honor their beliefs and minister to what they need as valuable souls without making anyone feel uncomfortable. I trust my intuition to help me know when to speak and when to remain silent on the subject. There is a time for everything.

It is important that I admit what I really believe because it is something that will benefit others. I would ask that if you don't embrace the idea of past lives or reincarnation, that for just a minute you consider the possibility that if a you can connect with the one-ness of God, that it might just be possible that you could connect with every life of every human being who ever lived, and a story from among all those life stories that is relevant to your own healing at the moment. That's the best way I can talk about soul healing with anybody. It may be the piece of truth that we will never quite know until our physical death.

You Have a Mission

We all have a mission that unfolds over time. Part of my mission was probably to raise children and learn to live within a world of science and business. I am certain that I chose that. When my children became older, I was able to move on to chapter two of my mission, which is about serving my clients, readers, audiences and the public with a greater awareness of the healing power of energy and the eternal nature of the soul.

Think about your mission and how you can be of highest service. Sometimes the clues to your mission have to do with choices that you've already made, things that you've felt very, very strongly about, and topics that get your attention and won't let you turn away. These are some of the clues!

Passion is one of those clues. Overcoming fear can be part of your mission, too. Why wouldn't overcoming that fear be part of accomplishing your mission as a higher consciousness being? My deep fear of becoming an acknowledged healer was something I was able to release through help from several experts, including an incredible live session I had on stage with EFT founder Gary Craig in 2008. I've now come to the place where I can publicly state that I am a healer without being afraid I'll be criticized, tortured or killed for it.

I've got two important questions for you today:

1. Can you list three or four things you are extremely, 100 percent passionate about?

2. If you asked your spouse or one of your best friends what your passions are, do they know? Could they answer correctly?

Passion is the way that we put our values out into the physical world. This is how each of us makes a difference. Passion is the energy that makes you who you are and allows you to accomplish important things in the world.

I'm challenging every single person to be more passionate. Let your energies shine and stop holding back the truth. If you have been dismissed, ignored, hurt or challenged because of your passion, take a step back. If you remain uncertain about your passions, there are some exercises in the Practice Time section at the end of this chapter to help you.

Searching for More

One of the principles I follow and continually teach is that we all have a right and responsibility to want more. Asking for more is the primary way to receive more, whether it occurs through thinking about our desires, dreaming, getting help, saying a prayer or writing a list of goals on a page. Coaching is a process that allows people to see the possibilities clearly and to formulate important plans for having and attracting more.

Being told to want more can stir up negative feelings. Perhaps those most uncomfortable with the concept don't feel worthy of more. They feel guilty for not being content with what they already have. I often remind my clients that it's possible to be filled with gratitude and appreciation, yet also desire more. The desire for more is our inner creator wanting to interact with the world. This is exactly how inventions, medical breakthroughs and miracles have occurred throughout history. As humans have dared to ask for something faster, safer, stronger, bigger or better—something new and useful is created. It is our Divine purpose to seek more and to allow God to respond. It is equally important that we humbly accept our gifts as the prayers for more are answered.

A world filled with deliberate creations of humans seeking more is a harmonious and peaceful place. Why not become part of it? Dare to dream, build, invent, write, plan and collaborate. There is more than enough to go around. Do your part in the big Divine plan. Live your mission by wanting more.

Child of Blessing, Child of Promise

I love attending the Sacrament Baptism at my church. It is a time of celebration when tiny babies are brought forward for the congregation and families to witness the vows of parents to be good teachers, the placement of holy water on their fragile heads and prayers of hope for the child to live in faith.

There is a particularly touching part of the ceremony at my church that brings tears to my eyes and a lump to my throat every time. After the official ceremony is completed, we sing a beautiful hymn called "Child of Blessing, Child of Promise." As the pastors carry these little babies down the center aisle of the church, each of our congregation members has a chance to gaze upon these tiny, precious individuals as we sing this song. There's something so beautiful about the beginning of a soul's mission in that pure, innocent form. Do these lyrics stir a lump in your throat too?

Child of Blessing, Child of Promise

Child of blessing, child of promise,
love's creation, love indeed!
Fresh from God, refresh our spirits,
into joy and laughter lead.

Child of joy, our dearest treasure,
God's you are, from God you came.
Back to God we humbly give you,
blessing you in Jesus' name.

Child of God, your loving Parent,
learn to know whose child you are.
Grow to laugh and sing and worship,
trust and love God more than all.

Words: ©1981 Ronald S. Cole-Turner
Tune: attributed to C.F. Witt, Psalmodia Sacra, 1715,
adapted by Henry J. Gauntlett, Hymns Ancient and Modern, 1861.

As the baby grows, learns from parents and has experiences, you may wonder if it's possible that that child chose specific parents to facilitate specific life lessons. Whether this soul chose outstanding parents or a situation of neglect and abuse, we must consider that either situation could contribute to a conscious soul lesson.

Life's mysteries remain. What we do know is that life continues to go on for decades, through adolescence, young adulthood, parenthood, middle age, grandparenthood and into those final years when we make our peace and transition beyond our physical body.

Recently I've enjoyed reading some amazing obituaries that remind me that each of us has a mission. Obituaries are a recollection of mission accomplished—what a soul was able to do between the moment of birth and the moment of death. Although obituaries are highlights based on the judgment of others, those judgments should reflect how well a person lived, loved, accomplished, and served the planet while they were here.

One of my favorite obituaries of all time is about a woman by the name of Ida Fisher Davidoff, age 97, who was a family therapy pioneer from New Canaan, Connecticut. The first few lines of Ida's obituary read as follows:

"Ida Fisher Davidoff died May 11, 2001 in New Canaan, Conn., where until recently she had baked her own bread, swum nude in her pool, and was 'always thinking ahead.' She was 97. She followed her own advice. When her four children grew up, she had 'a lovely depression' about her empty nest, then went back to college to earn a doctorate—at age 57—in marital and family counseling. When arthritis made it difficult to stoop over to tend her garden, she planted wildflowers in raised boxes. When her fingers got too stiff to play piano, she took singing lessons. She saw patients until a few weeks ago, and still planned to write a book, titled 'Age: A Work of Art,' using herself as her primary example."

Doesn't that obituary bring a vivid image of a spunky old lady to mind? Knowing that Ida certainly did so much more than was captured in this short summary, we can be fairly certain that she lived well.

Everybody can begin anew, with the end in mind by writing an obituary for themselves, going beyond goals. What impact will your life have? Are there things that you definitely want to accomplish before you die? Go for it! Tell other people what you're trying to do and enjoy the ride, just like Ida did.

Life Lessons

It never ceases to amaze me that just when I think I have figured out how a small particle of this universe works, something new comes along to show me how much more I still need to figure out. I guess I see this as a sign that there will always be a great reason to greet each new day as long as I'm here in physical form. As I strive to be a leader embracing enlightened stupidity, I will follow that humble, yet delightful path. I also realize that each one of us filters the messages from the Divine Source in very different ways, and that is how it should be. Each one of us is a true expression of that Divine energy, yet also someone who is unique in every sense of the word. That is the beauty of God's creation, to be recognized with a new awareness.

Writing has been a tough, uphill battle for me because I tend to be a perfectionist. I realize that so many people have already written important messages of spirituality, healing, balance and success. How could I possibly add something to these great written accomplishments? When I begin to wonder whether my voice could make any difference, I suddenly see that my unique nature can and will create something that has never been stated quite the same way before. That message will reach the souls who are ready to hear it, who are attracted to my frequency and it will reach them in a way that awakens something new within them.

It is my deliberate intention to be who I am. It is my wish for you, too. I'll be writing with new confidence and as I continue my journey beyond this book, I look forward to having kindred hearts respond to the messages you have received.

Life, Death and Transitions

We can choose to look at life as a series of transitions. Death is just another transition, a chapter of living that has ended, but a story not yet over. At death, the soul returns home, takes a break, reconnects with unlimited Source love and integrates the lessons learned. Ultimately the decision to return to the physical world in a new body with a new mission is one we choose as part of our soul growth.

Although I see death as a healthy, positive and a glorious transition, many people view it as a frightening unknown. I can recall specific clients who came to me living in guilt, bracing for judgment, and fearing that they would be rejected at the pearly gates of heaven. There were also clients who were angry at God and the church, or who hadn't been able to believe that there was anything more beyond this life. In either case, these poor people were holding onto life because that was all that they had to believe in.

As I've worked with these delicate souls so worried about death, I see how fear interferes with their ability to live and thrive. Those worries have detrimental effects on their health too. Fortunately, through coaching, spiritual counseling and energy healing tools, I've seen many find faith, emerge from worry and start living again. That is why I do what I do.

I admit that the possibility of losing someone I love, especially my closest family members, is something that fills me with sadness. Those losses will be deep, they'll hurt and they'll knock me down for a while. I also know loss is part of life. Death is part of the natural cycle. Love in its purest form is going to knock you down. Love is that strong, but you don't want to go through life without it. It's a beautiful part of our choice to be here.

Nobody wants to let go of something as precious as another being we love. Whether it's a child, an aging pet, a parent, friend or a spouse, we must instead hold on through the energetic connection and the belief that they remain, are with us after they go, and that someday we'll be with them again. That's what I believe. And I hope that you are able to find peace in some form of that belief, too.

The Indigo Connection

People often ask me how I came up with the name The Indigo Connection for my company. And I have to admit it was deliberate, but I don't talk about it very much. There was a time when I was pulling together a seminar and I was asked to address this. I really didn't have the words for it. Being somebody who journals often I decided to spend some time really mulling over the message, thinking it over in both my head and my heart so I had an answer to that question that could be shared and understood on many levels.

In my journal I wrote the following statement that I will share with you now.

> *"I am Indigo. The consciousness that translates the light*
> *and energy of God*
> *into the practical, physical world of human daily life.*
> *I am gentle as the night sky and as deep as the sea.*
> *A rare color in nature, possessed by only a few flowers and living*
> *creatures,*
> *ushering in a new age of being and consciousness."*

After I wrote this I stood back and gasped because this was a bigger definition for why I chose Indigo as part of my brand than I'd ever written down before. When I chose the name of the company I knew indigo was a beautiful blue color that I love and wear often and look great in. I also knew that indigo represented the third eye chakra and intuition. Indigo reflected my work as a coach, healer and helping professional who relies on intuition more and more every day.

I also liked indigo because it had the word "indi" within it, which brings to mind independence. That certainly was the case when I chose to become an entrepreneur. Indigo also contains the word "go," suggesting motion necessary for healthy energy as well as forward movement. Those of you who know me will agree that I rarely sit still for any length of time. I'm always on the go.

Finally, I have to admit I'm fascinated with the stories about The Indigo Children, these special little ones who have a sense of deep spirituality far beyond their years. I am indigo like them in that sense, too. Perhaps I tend to think there's some indigo in all of us waiting to be activated. A series of strange coincidences, people and experiences have activated the indigo in me. My understanding and identification with the indigo influence has always been with me, lying dormant beneath the surface.

Thoughts and ideas exist before they emerge into physical reality. Creativity is like that too. Creation is the birthing of something that already exists. Each soul is a birthing of something that already exists, yet is unique.

Be Contagious

You've already learned that your energy has a contagious nature allowing you to send signals out into the world so that you can change the world. When you send joy and love out to everything around you, others pick up on the vibrations and the frequencies of those high level emotions. People can be shifted so that they experience that same happy feeling that you're projecting. The same can be true for negative emotions. The good news is positive emotions have a much higher likelihood of reaching long distances with great intensity.

Be reminded that being contagious carries responsibility. It also helps if you take a few moments to set an intention before you go out there infecting the world. Your life mission helps you set those intentions. Know what you will spread. At the same time, what will you say "no" to so that you don't spread the wrong things around? That is how you live your mission and your purpose with deliberate intent, and so that your mission is accomplished. Just as giggling and uncontrollable laughter can be contagious, so can anything good and pure that you set your mind to. That's the power of contagious energy.

It's Not Over

If you're still struggling with the concepts of life and death, reincarnation, soul healing and anything else I've said in this chapter, I want to assure you that life is good and it continues infinitely. You are part of the infinite and there's never any end. Hold that thought in your heart.

I have learned in my work with clients releasing soul trauma, and helping earthbound spirits cross to the light, that there is a force of pull at that light that is familiar. I want to assure you that if there is someone who preceded you in death, who loved you strongly and for whom you still feel love, that individual will be there to meet you at that crossing place. A group of souls will be there whether you call or not, because that's how strong love is.

What about your beloved pets? I have lost many pets over the years and have found great comfort from the following poem:

The Rainbow Bridge

Just this side of heaven is a place called Rainbow Bridge.

When an animal dies that has been especially close to someone here, that pet goes to Rainbow Bridge.
There are meadows and hills for all of our special friends so they can run and play together.
There is plenty of food, water and sunshine, and our friends are warm and comfortable.

All the animals that had been ill and old are restored to health and vigor; those who were hurt or maimed are made whole and strong again, just as we remember them in our dreams of days and times gone by.
The animals are happy and content, except for one small thing; they each miss someone very special to them, who had to be left behind.

They all run and play together, but the day comes when one suddenly stops and looks into the distance. His bright eyes are intent; His eager body quivers. Suddenly he begins to run from the group, flying over the green grass, his legs carrying him faster and faster.

You have been spotted, and when you and your special friend finally meet, you cling together in joyous reunion, never to be parted again. The happy kisses rain upon your face; your hands again caress the beloved head, and you look once more into the trusting eyes of your pet, so long gone from your life but never absent from your heart.

Then you cross Rainbow Bridge together....

Author unknown

It's never over. And those reconnections and transitions are filled with love. Don't fear it. Look forward to it! Also know that those on the other side are there to support you, just as those orbs show up in photos now and then. Beings of light can be called to come to the edge, the fence between our side and theirs. I truly believe that the barrier separating our worlds is becoming thinner and that is to our great advantage as souls living on earth at this time.

You Are an Eternal Being

We are entering a new age. It is important to see yourself as a lasting, eternal being. There may be strife, pain and difficult situations, but know love prevails, that it's never over and that you are a powerful, limitless being who will live many lifetimes. Consciousness expands with each unpleasant thing that happens to you as well as each beautiful encounter of love. The consciousness of one contributes to the consciousness of all. Take your responsibilities seriously, reach for more and go in peace, living the mission that you've chosen to live.

I'm here to support you through your mission, struggles and triumphs. It is my honor to serve you and to continue serving you beyond this book.

I wish you a delightful life, everlasting!

Practice Time

1. Make a list of your values, making sure to include what you love. List 20 or 30 things. Go crazy. If you can come up with more, get them down on paper.

2. Think about times that you've been the most angry or most emotional. Use these memories as fuel to find passion, too. That's the dark side of passion. When you begin to find the true values behind those strong emotions, you'll learn a lot about yourself.

3. Find people who are passionate about the same things you love. Begin to make a list of supportive, passionate friends who can encourage and support you through your life mission. If you are having trouble identifying people for this list, instead make a list of qualities you are seeking in a supportive friend.

4. What do you want MORE of? When you start listing these things, do you feel any negative or unpleasant emotions? Do you experience joy in the thought? Treat the negative emotions with EFT tapping and amplify the positive feelings by vocalizing and tapping to affirmations.

5. Write your obituary. Include items you may not yet have accomplished, but dream of. Be creative, honest and optimistic. Share your obituary with loved ones, file it with your will, and then get back to living an inspired life.

6. Start thinking about who you know on the other side. Who do you want there to meet you when the time comes? Who might you want to begin an everlasting connection with now? There is no reason to wait.

Appendix I

Energy Self-Assessment

Rate each question as follows:

Always	5 Points
Most of the time	3 Points
Sometimes	2 Points
Never/No	0 Points

1. I feel focused, alert and safe when I am in a crowd or a large group.

2. I am free from control or manipulation at home and in my work place.

3. I am able to say "no" when I really should, without feeling guilty.

4. I am aware of my emotional state and my thoughts.

5. I am confident.

6. I can open up and let down my guard without fear of being hurt.

7. I easily let go of the past, forgive others and move on.

8. I am appropriately sensitive.

9. I live in the present moment.

10. It is easy for me to be honest and true to myself.

11. I sleep soundly and awaken refreshed.

12. I am attracted to foods that are healthy for me.

13. I am able to surrender and ask for help when life gets tough.

14. I have faith that I will live beyond my physical death.

15. I exercise at least 30 minutes each day.

16. I drink 8 or more glasses of pure water daily.

17. I limit my intake of sugar, salt and refined carbohydrates.

18. I experience comfortable digestion and elimination.

19. My body is comfortable and free of pain or irritation.

20. I believe a higher power interacts with my thoughts, intentions and prayers.

21. I am aware of my body's sensitivities and I honor them.

22. I move easily, with flexibility and with balance.

23. My skin is healthy and clear.

24. I look and feel younger than most people my age.

25. I have healthcare providers I trust.

26. I invite deeper connections in all areas of my work and life.

27. My waist/hip ratio (and that is the ratio of your wait measurement in inches divided by your hip measurement in inches) is approximately 0.7 if I'm a woman or 0.9 if I'm a man.

28. My body is good at giving me information and connecting me to intuition.

29. I am able to escape to magical places easily and often.

30. I breathe easily and fully.

Add up your score for each question

125-150   Congratulations, you are doing a great job managing your energy! Energy Makeover® affirms what you know plus more great tips.

90-124   You are doing okay, but could build consistently reliable comfort and stamina. Of course you want more!

50-89   You are just getting by, but have many things draining you. More energy is within your grasp! Energy Makeover® will rock your world.

0-49   Energy Crisis Alert! Energy Makeover® can radically improve your life. Get started ASAP.

Appendix II

Daily Energy Tracking Grid

Track Your Daily Energy Status

Check the box that indicates your status on a scale of 0 (depleted) to 10 (fully energized).

Day	Date	0	1	2	3	4	5	6	7	8	9	10	Comments*	Today's Self Care
1														
2														
3														
4														
5														
6														
7														
8														
9														
10														
11														
12														
13														
14														
15														
16														
17														
18														
19														
20														
21														
23														
24														
25														
26														
27														
28														
29														
30														

*Comment on stressors, diet, environment, emotions and any other relevant factor that might effect your energy status.

Appendix III

Betsy's Popular EFT
Self-Care Tapping Scripts

EFT for Difficult Relationships

Fill the blank with the name of a specific person

Set Up Statements *(rub sore spot or tap karate chop point)*

Even though I am powerless against _____'s negativity, I deeply love and accept myself.

Even though I never know how _____ will respond to me, I deeply love and accept myself.

Even though it doesn't feel safe to be me when I am around _____, I deeply love and accept myself;

I am firmly connected to infinite energy, allowing both of us to receive what we need.

I am grounded and protected. My boundaries are safe and solid;

I choose to remember I have the freedom and the right to say how I feel.

I choose to find safe and compassionate ways to communicate my needs and feelings.

I deserve to share my feelings in a way that respects _____ and my own dignity.

Tapping Statements – Negative Round:

I am powerless and alone. (top of head)

I can't say what I really think around _____ I'll cause trouble. (third eye)

I feel like they blame it on me. (eyebrow)

I feel disrespected and unappreciated. (side of eye)

I'm been silent for far too long. (under eye)

I've let _____ get to me too many times. (under nose)

It drains me to be in this relationship. (under lip)

Even if I speak up, _____ won't listen. (collarbone)

Why do I let this get to me? (underarm)

I'm angry when my needs are ignored. (under breast)

Tapping Statements – Positive Round:

I take the time to breathe before each encounter. (top of head)

I set a clear intention and intuitively know when and how to speak. (third eye)

I am committed to a compassionate approach when speaking up. (eyebrow)

My presence and voice are powerful and honest. (side of eye)

I trust that things are changing for the better. (under eye)

I stand up for myself safely. (under nose)

I can never be hurt when my intention is peace. (under lip)
I express my feelings without judgment. (collarbone)
I am heard. (under arm)
I offer my voice from a place of love. (under breast)

Tapping Statement – Mixed Round *(alternating negative and positive statements, always ending with a positive)*
I am a victim of a toxic relationship. (top of head)
I am able to honestly speak about what bothers me without hurting. (third eye)
I am distracted by the drama of the angry attack. (eyebrow)
I intend to remain safe and peaceful no matter what. (side of eye)
They deny me a chance to say what I need or feel. (under eye)
I am free and independent of their pull. (under nose)
They might pull me into the drama again. (under lip)
I am strong, compassionate and protected. (collarbone)
There's nothing I can say or do. (under arm)
I create positive energy in this relationship—and I am strong enough to affect a positive outcome. (under breast)

EFT for Forgiveness

Set Up Statements (rub sore spot or tap karate chop point)

Even though I have been holding on to this hurt for so long, I deeply love and accept myself.

Even though forgiveness feels so wrong when I've been hurt so deeply, I deeply love and accept myself.

Even though I am not able to let this go and move on, I deeply love and accept myself as I am.

I choose to realize that this happened, it is over and I am safe now.

I deserve to let this go so that I can heal these wounds and get on with my life

I choose to forgive myself for holding onto this unpleasant memory for so long

I request Divine Grace so that my spirit can release this painful memory.

I am sorry this happened and I release you by from my energy now.

Tapping Statements – Negative Round:

I can't seem to let this go. (top of head)

The memory is still so intense and painful. (third eye)

I want you to suffer. (eyebrow)

I am still powerless when it comes to what happened. (side of eye)

If I forgive you, you get away with it. (under eye)

Victims can't forgive. (under nose)

This is too big to forgive. (under lip)

What happens when I finally let this go? (collarbone)

I must keep fighting even though it's over (underarm)

I'm too angry to forgive this. (under breast)

Tapping Statements – Positive Round:

I am ready to feel better (top of head)

What you did was wrong, but I don't have to hold on to this anymore. (third eye)

I can see life lessons through my pain (eyebrow)

Time has helped me forgive you (side of eye)

I am sorry for you (under eye)

I forgive you. (under nose)

I completely forgive you (under lip)

I deserve to forgive you and be free at last (collarbone)

My words of forgiveness make a difference. (under arm)

I offer my forgiveness from a place of love. (under breast)

Tapping Statements – Mixed Round (alternating negative and positive statements, always ending with a positive)

I am a victim and I am hurting (top of head)

I forgive you with a loving heart (third eye)

I have been drained by this too long (eyebrow)

I can be peaceful as I forgive this (side of eye)

My sense of faith has been shaken by this (under eye)

Forgiveness is my way of taking charge again. (under nose)

What if I get caught up in the drama again? (under lip)

I have already handled enough. I am strong enough to let this go. (collarbone)

I wonder if I can completely release this? (under arm)

I allow God's grace to work a forgiveness miracle for me. (under breast)

EFT for Life Change in the Midst of Fear

Set Up Statements (rub sore spot or tap karate chop point)

Even though I don't know what to change, I don't know where to focus my attention, and I don't know which change will bring me the greatest benefit, I choose to let go of this confusion and choose change from my heart. My heart will know what is best for me, because
I completely love and accept myself.

Even though I'm not sure what I'm going to change, I know I desire change. Change is hard.
It's okay for me to change. I choose tiny changes so I can be gentle on myself because I completely love and accept myself.

Even though I'm scared to make changes because it is all uncertain, I'm going to choose to make some good changes. I believe it is worth the risk. I accept positive intentions and make these changes because I completely love and accept myself.

Tapping Statements:

I bring in my Higher Power to inspire me. (top of head)

My intuition selects appropriate changes. (third eye)

There is nothing to fear—change can be deliberate, positive and intentional. (eyebrow)

This is an easy process for me. There are so many changes I want. (side of eye)

I trust that change will make a difference for me. (under eye)

I choose many changes and they are all easy. (under nose)

I'm going to write down my changes so that they will happen. (under lip)

I'm going to pick one of these changes and begin today. (collarbone)

I can amaze myself with the power of change. (under arm)

I am excited about the changes. I'm excited about getting what I ask for. (under breast)

EFT for Overcoming Weight Loss Resistance

Setup Statements (rub sore spot in circular motion or tap karate chop point)

Even though I don't want to eat less and give up my favorite foods, I deeply love and accept myself.

Even though I feel deprived when I diet, I deeply love and accept myself.

Even though I can't even lose weight when I do diet, I deeply love and accept myself.

I choose to be a free, fit and satisfied person who takes care of me.

I choose to believe the positive words I create in my mind.

I choose to see myself successful this time because I deserve it and know it is safe and healthy for me.

Tapping Statements – Negative Round:

I am obsessed with my next meal. (top of head)

My thoughts focus on foods I'm not supposed to have. (third eye)

I am totally distracted by cravings and hunger. (eyebrow)

Only sweet, fat and salt will satisfy me. (side of eye)

My obsessive chocolate craving. (under eye)

Looking for my next snack. (under nose)

Hiding my snacks so nobody knows. (under lip)

Searching for satisfaction. (collarbone)

Craving something that disrupts my health. (under arm)

Lost in my cycle of food (under breast)

Tapping Statements – Positive Round:

Contented and breathing. (top of head)

My thoughts focus on my health and body. (third eye)

I am committed to caring for my body. (eyebrow)

Activities and friends are more valuable than food. (side of eye)

I choose healthy behavior, without distraction. (under eye)

I find something better I can do with this energy. (under nose)

I am focused on my commitment to me. (under lip)

Freedom is something I use responsibly. (collarbone)

My highest intentions always win. (under arm)

I am healthier and lighter from my deliberate behavior now and in every year to come. (under breast)

Tapping Statements – Mixed Round (alternating negative and positive statements, always ending with a positive)
I am a food addict. (top of head)
I am able to relax and allow the cravings to drift away. (third eye)
My salt and sugar obsessions disturb my peace. (eyebrow)
I have found surprising strength to resist effortlessly. (side of eye)
I'm messed up before and given in to my cravings. (under eye)
I'm not sure I can really resist this time. (under nose)
Of course I can resist. I'm in charge of me! (under lip)
Freedom is something I use responsibly. (collarbone)
My cravings get the best of me. (under arm)
I can do this! I am willing to lose the inches and uncover my true beauty. (under breast)

EFT to Heal Chronic, Unreasonable Cravings

Setup Statements (rub sore spot in circular motion or tap karate chop point)

Even though I am so anxious that I must medicate with food, I deeply love and accept myself.

Even though I eat too quickly and don't even realize what I'm feeding my body, I deeply love and accept myself.

Even though I'm sabotaging my efforts at health and weight loss with my private food frenzy, I deeply love and accept myself.

I choose to be satisfied and content with just enough food to nourish my body.

I choose to be present in each bite.

I ask for divine willpower and strength to break my cycle of addiction and to steer me to foods that restore wholeness.

Tapping Statements – Negative Round:

I'm out of control. (top of head)

I'm stuck in the momentum of eating. (third eye)

I 'm overcome by anxiety and haunted by food. (eyebrow)

I hide this unhealthy behavior and I'm ashamed of it. (side of eye)

I've been stuck with a bottomless pit. (under eye)

I don't even think before I eat. (under nose)

I eat without stopping. (under lip)

I eat all night. (collarbone)

I'm trapped repeating this cycle over and over again. (under arm)

There's something missing and I eat to fill the space. (under breast)

Tapping Statements – Positive Round:

I am a peaceful and mindful eater. (top of head)

I savor each bite and slow down to fully appreciate my blessings. (third eye)

My intention of health allows me greater awareness at all times. (eyebrow)

I make powerful, peaceful choices to restore wholeness. (side of eye)

I am ready to heal the emotions connected to my wild cravings. (under eye)

I write down how I feel and open up to greater love and understanding. (under nose)

My choices are making a positive difference. (under lip)

I am at peace with my body. (collarbone)
This is easier than I expected it to be. (under arm)
I have found my strength. (under breast)

Tapping Statements – Mixed Round (alternating negative and positive statements, always ending with a positive)

I am a victim of chronic food obsession. (top of head)
I am able to eat in a mindful and deliberate way. (third eye)
Cravings just happen at my age. (eyebrow)
I don't have to buy that—I've changed and I'm in charge now. (side of eye)
I feel guilty for this behavior. (under eye)
I forgive myself for thinking I don't matter. (under nose)
This chronic problem is too hard to heal. (under lip)
I can be free! I can deliberately have less stress and more peace. (collarbone)
I'm not important and I don't matter anyway. (under arm)
I matter! I'm here for a reason. I honor my health is part of my mission. (under breast)

EFT for Easing Procrastination and Fear

Set Up Statements (Tapping side of hand or sore spot)
Even though I am an outrageous procrastinator, I love and accept myself today, right now.
Even though I put off what I could do immediately and what I need to do soon, it's okay, I love and accept myself today.
Even though I drag my feet and put up all sorts of excuses when I could just take action, it's all right. I love and accept myself today.
I choose to be a person of action.
I choose to take that first small step to gain momentum toward my goal.
I choose to be clear and focused about what I need to accomplish and be gentle on myself as I go forward.
I choose this for myself because I love and accept myself today.

Tapping Statements:
I call upon all of my resources to inspire and assist me in the process of action. (top of head)
I trust myself and allow my higher intelligence to guide the process that I need. (third eye)
I release the fears and doubts about previous problems I have had in getting started and getting motivated. (eyebrow)
I forgive myself for the times I didn't take action when I could have. (side of eye)
I trust that today is different. I trust that I can begin and really get into my activities and complete them ahead of schedule. (under eye)
I stand up and take that first step. That is the important part. (under nose)
My body responds to my suggestions. I am filled with energy, optimism and enthusiasm. (under lip)
I love that I can create today and can create something worthwhile and of service to others. (collarbone)
I embrace all that I am, all that I have learned and all that I know to accomplish something really good today. (under arm)
I celebrate my successes, my triumphs with each new step as I move toward my goal and my life purpose. I am a person of action. (under breast)

EFT for Faith in the Midst of Uncertainty

Setup Statements (rub sore spot in circular motion or tap karate chop point)

Even though I still find myself in fear at times, it's okay.
    I love and accept myself and I choose to have FAITH.
Even though I get wrapped up in ego-trips and controversy and confrontation, it's all right.
    I love and accept myself now and I choose to be a creator of peace.

Even though there are times when it is dark and "nothing" is happening,
    I love and accept myself anyway and I choose to remember the light is just around the corner.

I choose to trust my Creator.
I choose to let go of my attachments and allow what IS to take place.
I choose all that I deserve.
I choose to create safely and in a healthy way.
My identity is strengthened when I am a creator.
My artistic talents are contagious.

Tapping Statements:

I trust my connection to ALL THERE IS. (top of head)
My intuition guides me every single moment of every day. (third eye)
I can spend quiet time with my Creator and find comfort in the stillness. (eyebrow)
I forgive myself for worrying and doubting. (side of eye)
I receive with gladness. I do so much with what I get. (under eye)
I have fun watching my ideas take physical form. (under nose)
I attract joyful souls into my life. These are my companion artists for dream sharing. (under mouth)
I face all things knowing that I never walk alone. (collarbone)
I am always connected and always safe. I am eternal and everlasting. (under arm)
I appreciate the beauty and the freedom I have at my disposal. I use these gifts wisely (under breast)

Repeat multiple times, as needed

EFT for Healing the Blocked Creator

Setup Statements (rub sore spot in circular motion or tap karate chop point)

Even though I'm not good enough yet and I don't consider myself the best creator,
  It's okay, I'm working on it and I love and accept myself anyway.

Even though I'm not getting paid for my creativity like I think I should be,
  It's okay, I'm hopeful and I choose to love and accept myself anyway.

Even though I've taken nasty criticism to heart and it hurt me and shut me down sometimes,
  It's okay. I love and accept myself anyway.
I choose to let all this go and open myself up to creation.
I am a co-creator.
Spirit works through and in creation.
There are no mistakes.
I am part of a miracle.

Tapping Statements:

I call upon a Higher Power to release the Creator within me. (top of head)
I am successful and prolific as a co-creator. (third eye)
I make a living doing what I love every single day. (eyebrow)
I'm creating a life that reflects what's dear to my heart. (side of eye)
I have all the money I need. Spirit is supporting me. (under eye)
I am so rich, I have much to share. (under nose)
I have arrived at a place where I am secure. (under mouth)
Criticism and judgment does not affect me. I am the judge and I love and accept myself completely. (collarbone)
I am publishing, creating and selling. The world needs what I do. (under arm)
I forgive myself for feeling scared before. I am brave NOW. I am a brave creator who enjoys the process. (under breast)

EFT for Strengthening Identity as a Creative Being

Setup Statements (rub sore spot in circular motion or tap karate chop point)

Even though I'm still searching for my true identity, I deeply and completely love and accept myself right now.

Even though I've been plagued with crazy-makers and people who have installed doubts into my system, I deeply and completely accept myself anyway and forgive myself for being so negative.

Even though I've denied who I really am in an effort to please others, I admit it. I love and accept myself for who I am right now, and forgive the people who made me see myself as anything less than a beautiful child of God.

I choose to take care of my artist child.

I choose to create a supportive environment for her/him.

I choose to be the caregiver for this sacred, creative child. I will do it well, always from a place of love.

Tapping Statements:

I call upon a higher power to help me with the challenges. (top of head)

I am inspired by my inner wisdom and brave enough to follow it. (third eye)

I have time, space and permission to be me, and when I do I thrive. (eyebrow)

I forgive myself for shutting down and letting myself become blocked. (side of eye)

I can be trusted with a crayon, paint or pencils. I boldly color outside of the lines. (under eye)

As a creator I am free, confident and extremely safe. (under nose)

I am comfortable with my power to create. (under mouth)

I am constantly in touch with my own inner truth and this material is outstanding. (collarbone)

I am filled with a better knowing of myself than I have ever experienced before. (under arm)

I deal with my feelings. As I become a lighter and freer soul, my joy is contagious (under breast)

Tap sides of ankles if you like to help move and ground the energy flow.

Say the following affirmations aloud as you do heart massage or tap the
   EFT points:

Affirmations to Lock in the Healing

I have chosen to be the strong and creative person I was created to be.
As I claim my purpose, I live fully in harmony with my world.

EFT for Attracting Abundance in ALL Ways

Setup Statements (rub sore spot in circular motion or tap karate chop point)

Even though I am guilty for wasting and squandering the money I have, and sometimes forget how I have spent it, I deeply and completely love and accept myself today.

Even though I limit my definition of abundance and my belief in my ability to have more, I deeply and completely love and accept myself today, exactly as I am right now.

Even though I forget how rich I am at present and I miss so many of the riches that have come into my life and exist in my life right now, I forgive myself for this and I love and accept myself anyway.

I choose to be highly aware of all the abundance that I have attracted up to this present moment.

I choose to shift my thinking and expand my imagination to include abundance that may have seemed out of reach in the past.

I choose to admire abundance and to collect images and symbols of abundance.

I choose to play games that allow me to flex my abundance muscles because I deserve more, it is possible for me to have more and I attract more.

All of this is healthy for me, healthy for my family and healthy for everyone who touches my life.

I accept abundance without guilt. I share abundance liberally and I turn abundance into wonderful memories because I am present, conscious and using what the universe has provided me.

Tapping Statements:

I am grateful for all that comes into my world and I credit a higher power for listening to my desires. (top of head)

I am exceptional at seeing possibilities. I am stretching my imagination to include financial and experiential abundance. (third eye)

I am cared for. I never worry about money because I always have enough. (eye brow)

I forgive myself for the times I took my spending for granted. That time is over. (side of eye)

I can be trusted with lots of money. I can be trusted with more money than I have now. I use money well. (under eye)

My investments bring exceptional returns. I always increase the value of what I have. (under nose)

I care for the things I have extremely well. I am a caretaker of abundance. (under mouth)

My abundance appreciates over time. I know what I value. The things I hold on to increase in value. I have so much to share. (collarbone)

I am able to see abundance in all ways and in every sense I possess. (under arm)

I teach others about abundance through my example. I am a steward and an exceptional expert in creating abundance. (under breast)

Appendix IV

Recommended Resources for Further Study

Books:

A New Earth by Eckhart Tolle. Dutton, 2005.

Ancient Secret of the Fountain of Youth by Peter Kelder. Doubleday, 1998.

Ask and It Is Given by Esther and Jerry Hicks. Hay House Inc., 2004.

BACKWARDS: Returning to Our Source for Answers by Nanci I Danison, A.P. Lee & Co., 2007.

Destiny of Souls by Michael Newton, PhD. Llewellyn Publications, 2001.

EFT for Weight Loss by Gary Craig. Energy Psychology Press, 2010.

Endless Energy by Debra Greene, PhD. MetaComm Media, 2009.

Energy Medicine for Women by Donna Eden. The Penguin Group, 2008.

Energy Psychology Interactive by David Feinstein PhD. Innersource, 2004.

Everyday Bliss for Busy Women by Maryam Webster, M.Ed. New Harbinger Publications, 2008.

Freedom at Your Fingertips by Ronald E. Ball. Inroads Publishing, 2006.

Journey of Souls by Michael Newton, PhD. Llewellyn Publications, 1994.

Orbs Their Mission and Messages of Hope by Klaus Heinemann and Gundi Heinemann, Hay House, Inc., 2010.

Powerful Statements for Everyday Healing by Betsy Muller. Indigo Connection Press, 2009.

Reaching Further: How to remove obstacles to personal excellence by John Hartung, PsyD. Colorado School of Professional Psychology, 2005.

Take Time for Your Life by Cheryl Richardson. Broadway Books, 1998.

Tapping Into Creativity by Betsy Muller. Indigo Connection Press, 2009.

The Artist's Way by Julia Cameron. Penguin Putnam Inc., 1992.

The Art of Extreme Self-Care by Cheryl Richardson. Hay House Inc., 2001.

The Bond by Lynne McTaggart. Free Press, 2011.

The EFT Manual by Gary Craig. Energy Psychology Press, 2008.

The Power of Focus by Jack Canfield, Mark Victor Hanson and Les Hewitt, Health Communications, 2000.

The True Power of Water by Masaru Emoto. Beyond Words Publishing Inc., 2005.

Vibrational Medicine by Richard Gerber, MD. Bear and Company, 2001.

Winning at Waist Management by Betsy Muller. Indigo Connection Press, 2010.

You Can Heal Your Life by Louise Hay. Hay House Inc., 1994.

Websites:

Directory of Feng Shui Practitioners www.fengshuidirectory.com

Emotional Freedom Techniques www.eftuniverse.com

Jazzercise www.jazzercise.com

Joseph Mercola, DO www.mercola.com

Rick Steeves www.ricksteeves.com

The Indigo Connection theindigoconnection.com

Weight Watchers www.weightwatchers.com

Websites of Recommended Practitioners, Professionals and Coaches:

Cara Gallagher, Feng Shui Consultant www.Caragallagher.com

Mary Giuseffi http://www.sparklecommunications.com

Cheryl Leuthaueser, DO http://integrativewellcare.com

Isam Nemeh, MD http://drnemeh.com

Tenpenny Integrative Medical Center, Sherri Tenpenny, DO
www.osteomed2.com

Dawn Waldrop www.best-impressions.com

Barbara Stone, PhD www.souldetective.net

Organizations

The Association for Comprehensive Energy Psychology
www.energypsych.org

The Certified Energy Coach Program www.certifiedenergycoach.org

The Cleveland Coach Federation www.clevelandcoachfederation.org

The International Society for the Study of Subtle Energies and Energy
Medicine www.issseem.org

NSA Ohio - Ohio Speakers Association www.nsaohio.com

Energy Medicine and Energy Psychology www.innersource.net

The Heart Math Institute www.heartmath.com

About The Author

Betsy Muller is a coach, speaker, healer and author. After decades working in a variety of traditional business and healthcare management settings, life changed in 2001 when she discovered energy psychology techniques at a conference in Switzerland. Since then, her passion has been to help others enjoy balanced and purposeful lives by integrating positive energy flow into life and business applications.

She combines her gifts as an intuitive coach, captivating speaker and energy health practitioner with over 30 years of business experience to help her clients thrive amidst the dynamic balance of work, home, relationships, finances, health and spiritual consciousness. Her company, The Indigo Connection, offers private and group coaching, networking programs, retreats, training in holistic coaching techniques, consulting for holistic service businesses, inspirational keynotes and conference workshops.

Betsy is the 2nd person in the world to become a Certified Energy Health Practitioner (CEHP) though the Association for Comprehensive Energy Psychology. Betsy is also Ohio's first Certified Energy Coach (CEC), an Intermediate Certified EFT (Emotional Freedom Techniques) Practitioner and an ordained minister.

Ms. Muller holds a BA in Chemistry from The College of Wooster and a MBA in Systems Management from Baldwin Wallace College. Betsy is the mother of two adult children and lives in Northeast Ohio with her husband George and beloved pets Gracie, Sig and Pepper.

Contact the author by visiting her on the web at
www.theindigoconnection.com and www.energymakeover4U.com

Keep Your Energy Makeover® Going!

- Contact Betsy to speak at your next conference or event by calling 440-238-4731

- Join the Energy Makeover® Mailing List at www.EnergyMakeover4u.com

- Send your Energy Makeover® stories to betsy@theindigoconnection.com

- Order *Winning at Waist Management*™ by Betsy Muller on Amazon Kindle

CPSIA information can be obtained at www.ICGtesting.com
Printed in the USA
BVOW012253110313

315280BV00007B/20/P

9 781935 723424